Please
Return

COVENANT
NURSERY
SCHOOL

BOOKS BY T. BERRY BRAZELTON, M.D.

Infants and Mothers
Toddlers and Parents
On Becoming a Family
Doctor and Child
To Listen to a Child
Working and Caring
What Every Baby Knows
Families: Crisis and Caring

Families
Crisis and Caring

❧

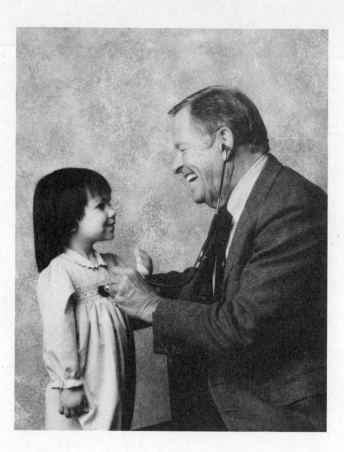

Families
Crisis and Caring

❧

T. BERRY BRAZELTON, M.D.

Ballantine Books • New York

To Ellen

"Whatever does not specifically back up the idea that parents are responsible people will in the long run be harmful to the very core of society. . . . Out of the healthy family comes the future."

D. W. Winnicott
*The Child, the Family,
and the Outside World*

The publishers wish to thank Nancy Poland, R.N., for providing background material vital to the preparation of the manuscript, and for helping to coordinate continuing communication with the families whose lives are portrayed in this book.

We are also grateful to Peggy Lamont and her colleagues at Tomorrow Entertainment, not only for initiating "What Every Baby Knows," the wonderful cable series which inspired this book – as well as an earlier book which carried the same name as the show – but also for generously making available videotapes, transcripts, and other materials.

Finally, we wish to thank Joelle Delbourgo, Vice-President and Editor-in-Chief of Ballantine Books' trade paperbacks, whose vision it was to bring the true stories in the cable series to the reading public.

Contents

Introduction

ฆ

This is a book about real families and the ways they have handled major challenges and crises. For all parents, creating and raising a family consist of one adjustment after another. The ways that strong, healthy families handle these adjustments, whether large ones – adoption, serious illness, divorce – such as those described in this book, or small, predictable ones – teething, the first step, a new baby sitter – follow certain patterns. These universal patterns – of turmoil, regression, reorganization, and growth – can be seen in the families which have courageously and generously shared their experiences with me and with the reader. In their stories we can see how the highs of parenting grow from conquering the low points, and how without the process of trial and error these families would not be as strong today.

All parents worry about making mistakes. Not only are mistakes unavoidable, however, but parents learn their job through mistakes. One reason it can be difficult for successful working parents to adapt to child rearing is that the culture of the workplace is often one of perfectionism and of dependable rewards. In raising a family, on the other hand, rewards are rarely dependable, although they are all the more joyous because of their unpredictability. Perfectionism and the systematic pursuit of success have no place in parenting.

The families in this book have all had to face special and serious kinds of stress. Not every family will face these problems, but all families will have feared or dreamed about them. The opportunity we have to identify with these actual mothers and fathers as they overcome their difficulties is their gift to us.

As Robin and Chris Cutler acknowledge their feelings of rivalry in the intense relationships that characterize their family – rivalry with each other and with their adopted son's magical grandmother – they uncover feelings which all of us face as we become a family. The Humphreys family is a successful stepfamily. In their story, the issues with which a stepchild and stepparent must deal come into clear perspective. Since nearly half the children in the United States are now being raised in stepfamilies, it becomes more and more critical to understand the way actual families handle these relationships. Rather than simply lamenting the statistics, or constructing rosy theories about that modern-day fantasy, the "blended family," we must look at real stepfamilies. As with many of the problems faced in this book, the more openly they are faced, the more turmoil and new issues emerge, and the greater likelihood a strong new family will be forged.

The O'Connell-Beder family uncovers the wrenching issues which couples face when they find they are unable to conceive and bear their own children and are labeled infertile. The transition to caring for the children of others, particularly in a cross-cultural adoption, is not easy, but it can be made rewarding and exciting. Eileen and Barry's experience with their Korean daughter, Jenny, raises the universal question – how much is nature (inherited), how much is nurture?

Especially difficult situations face the Coopers and the McClays. The Cooper children have lost their mother. Their father, a policeman, is suddenly a single parent, coping with a teenage daughter's feelings as well as those of a four-year-old son. The way they gradually draw strength from their tragedy is illuminating. The McClays and their son Kevin have faced three years of his leukemia – the shock of diagnosis and the burdens of treatment. Their insights, as they face this life-threatening illness with him and with his siblings, moved and astonished me.

All of these families were candid about their deeper feelings. Their responses to stress differ enormously, though a universal pattern can be seen. I hope I have communicated both the lessons these parents and children taught me and my admiration for each one of them.

All five families originally appeared with me on the cable TV show "What Every Baby Knows," from which the stories and questions in this book are adapted. An earlier book, with the same title as the show, portrayed five other families facing more common, everyday joys and problems of life with children. I have never enjoyed writing anything as much as the profiles and dialogues in that book and those that follow.

I would again like to thank the many people who made the cable shows, and my profound experiences with these families, possible. John Backe and Peggy Lamont, founders of Tomorrow Entertainment, gave me the opportunity to participate in the making of the cable television series. Because of their vision, and the talents of Lou Gorfain, Chuck Bangert, and Hank O'Karma of New Screen Concepts, the power of the visual medium was added to insights into child development which I've long tried to convey in writing. Procter and Gamble generously sponsored this innovative programming, thanks to the enthusiasm and hard work of Beverly O'Malley and Erika Gruen of Saatchi and Saatchi. The staff of the Child Development Unit at Children's Hospital in Boston, and especially Nancy Poland, an experienced pediatric nurse practitioner and mother of three daughters, helped strengthen the content of the shows, using the background of our years of research together. Nancy's deep understanding of parents and their concerns made possible the atmosphere of trust and candor in which the shows were filmed and the books were written.

Neither the cable shows nor the books would have been possible without the parents themselves: Robin and Chris Cutler, Charles Cooper, Liz and Howie Humphreys, Valerie and Kevin McClay, Eileen O'Connell and Barry Beder. My gratitude to them and to their splendid children cannot be fully conveyed.

The Cutler
Family

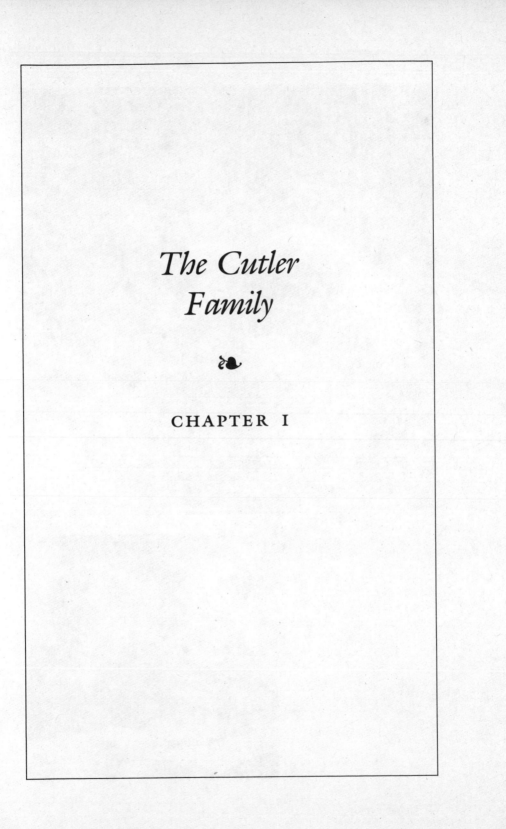

CHAPTER I

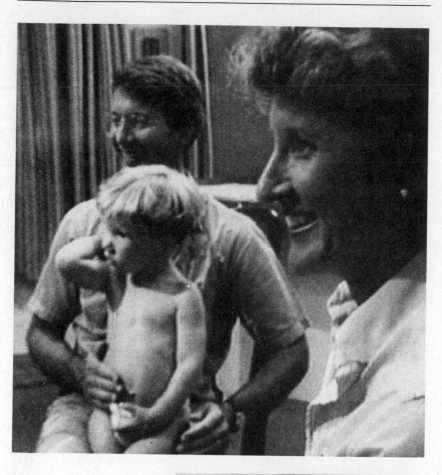

The Cutler Family

The Cutler Family

Family History

ह०

Robin and Christopher Cutler are both Yankees. Chris, thirty-eight, comes from an established Boston family; he is blond, athletic, and self-assured. He is also affable, winning everyone with his ready smile and easy charm. His son, Wiley, sixteen months old, is obviously very attached to him. During our visit, Wiley rarely left his father's knee, watching my face whenever I talked to Chris.

Robin, thirty-six, is dark, chic, and also self-assured. A successful interior designer, she drives forty miles in and out of Boston from their home near Worcester several times a week to consult. She is much sought after and commands sizable fees. Robin is very articulate and also spontaneous. One has the feeling of instant communication with her. I felt close to her right away. Her almost childlike lack of inhibitions contrasts with the image of style and competence which she also projects.

Chris recently changed jobs, from that of a management consultant to an administrative post at a local hospital. He made the change in order to have more time at home with Wiley. He explained that he could see Wiley's childhood slipping away as he commuted to work for long hours and traveled around the Northeast, often away overnight. He recalled his relationship with his own father, who also commuted long hours. He'd grown up longing to know his father better, and refused to repeat this with Wiley. Hence, he had quickly reacted to Wiley's arrival by searching out employment close to home, making sure that he would have at least part of every day with his family.

The fourth vital member of this family is Robin's mother. Left a widow with three small children, she went to work to support them and became a much-admired teacher in a fine old private school in Boston. She was able to raise the children, put them through college, and see them established in successful careers before she retired a few years ago. Now in her sixties, she is energetic, elegant, and captivating. She has remained very close to her daughter. Wiley is enraptured by her. I was too, and watched the delightful and imaginative way she mothered everyone in this family.

When I first met this family Chris talked to me openly about his childhood longing for more time with his father – time which went to his father's profession, architecture. Chris's father worked hard, was successful, and provided his sons with excellent educations and an example of dedication to a career. He worked and played equally hard on the weekends: clearing woods, tennis, running, and teaching his sons endurance and agility. But his devotion to work created a distance and an unfulfilled longing in Chris. Despite these feelings, it was obvious that his father had raised him well. For Chris is a warm, masculine man, both nurturing and firm. He is determined to change the pattern of fathering with Wiley.

Wiley is adopted. Robin and Chris were married for five years before they started to plan a family. At that point, they expected to be able to conceive right away. Robin had a miscarriage soon after they started trying. After that miscarriage, nothing more happened. "It didn't take us long to know we were in trouble," said Robin. "Each month, our anxiety built up. We went through all the horrors of an infertility workup. I was determined to have children and so was Chris. We each needed it for ourselves, but also as a couple; we needed a child to share. At first, our friends asked whether we were ever going to try. When we tried to answer them honestly, they usually became uncomfortable and changed the subject. It was as if we had a disease. Each of us tried to take the blame, to protect the other – as if it were someone's fault. Yet there was no medical diagnosis, just 'infertility, cause unknown.' Everyone in our family got into the act. They sent us articles on infertility. We learned that 15 to 20 percent of all couples are infertile. That was reassuring. At least others had the same problem. Forty to 45 percent of the problem is from the male; the rest is due to the female. We started to feel very alone at family gatherings, wanting to join our brothers' and sisters' little children with our own. We were running on empty. We felt a huge chasm every time we saw the others. We have tried now for eight years, and we had to give up or try something else to save our sanity. The biological clock was pushing me – I'm already over thirty-five, so we had to do something."

"We were determined to get a Caucasian child," said Chris, "although everyone told us we couldn't do it. We began to make a full-time search for a white child. We went public. We told everyone we met, 'We want a baby.' All our friends began to scout for us. We found one lawyer in New York who wanted $15,000 cash for a baby. Eventually, we were referred to a lawyer in South Carolina who worked exclusively on adoptions. Through a system where the natural parents and prospective adopting parents can make contact and discuss the situation, the emotional side of the arrangement is initiated. Then the lawyer steps in to handle the legal aspects for his usual fee. Once we found the natural parents, we waited only two weeks. But before that time, we had put in eight months of intensive work, especially on Robin's part, in developing our network. We immediately wondered what the catch was, whether the mother was healthy or not, what would be wrong with the baby. We never questioned but that something would be. Otherwise, it would be too good to be true. Our lawyer met the girl, then proceeded to make the medical, hospital, and legal arrangements. We flew down to get our baby, sight unseen. What an act of faith! I still couldn't believe it and looked for things wrong with him. When he opened his eyes on the airplane home, they were crossed. I yelled for the stewardess and asked her to look. She said, well, how old is he? I forgot in my panic and said, 'I don't know. I hardly know him.' All of our talk woke him up, and his eye straightened out. What fools we were. By the time we got home, we were completely in love."

Robin wanted to tell the rest of the story. "I felt I had to adopt. I had to stop grieving about my failure. Adoption was a way out. And it is! I think adoptive parents have an even stronger kind of love to offer. We *need* them so much. And we need to prove ourselves. Of course, we also need to have them turn out perfectly. And Wiley was – from the first. He was the miracle we'd been waiting for. We felt such a deep love right away. Underneath the magic there is a sense that the bubble might burst.

"We made only one call, from the airport, telling a neighbor about our trip, but it seemed as though the whole town was ready.

The Cutler Family

When we arrived home we found that they had gotten into our house and had set up a complete, working nursery for Wiley's homecoming. How's that for part of the miracle? We walked in to have everybody cheering and drinking champagne. And we could show off this gorgeous creature!"

Robin's eyes had reddened, and she paused to look over at Wiley. "From the beginning," she went on, "we seemed to know Wiley. He just came easy. Although we had a hard time adjusting to adoption, he helped us. We had been through so much, getting checked out for everything that might be wrong with us. Every time, they'd send us home, saying, 'Just go home and make a baby. You're normal.' What a farce! We tried and tried. Each of us felt we were failing the other. Our marriage was really being stressed."

Robin's mother then spoke up. "I was so concerned about Robin's mental well-being. Do you believe in miracles? I do. I went to church on the first Sunday in Advent. I prayed to send her a baby. The baby was born that day!"

"From the moment we got him," said Chris, "I felt I knew him, as though he were part of me. It was hard to concentrate on my work any longer. I had to be at home with him. He was amazing. I had to watch everything he did. I was in love! I knew I didn't want to repeat my father's workaholism and his remoteness from us as little boys. I just didn't want to miss out on Wiley. I began to spend every available moment with him. I was so re-warded and fulfilled that my career, I realized, was going to take a back seat to this baby. My new job close by allowed me tremendous time with Wiley and also with Robin – we had waited so long to share this joy."

The Involved Father

えル

OFFICE VISIT

Chris brought Wiley in to see me for a vaccination, a routine visit.

DR. BRAZELTON　Just you and Wiley today? How are you both?

CHRIS　Wiley is terrific. I'm balancing work and Wiley.

DR. BRAZELTON　Can you spend much time at home?

CHRIS　Quite a bit, even though the job takes a lot of focus and energy.

DR. BRAZELTON　It's a tough time for any man, but seeing the way Wiley looks up at you and clings to you shows how important this time has been for him. I suspect it is for you, too.

CHRIS　People told us when he was a little baby that if we talked to him a lot and really paid attention to him, the payback would come early and strong, and it has. It's really gratifying. When I was growing up, my dad worked very long hours and I didn't see him a heckuva lot. I don't want that — for me or for Wiley. I missed my dad. When we were with him, it was very intense, so my feelings of missing him were magnified.

DR. BRAZELTON　You mean your relationship was either/or —

CHRIS　Yes, he was gone or he was there. *While speaking Chris is looking at Wiley.*

The Cutler Family

DR. BRAZELTON Does being with Wiley give you any memories or a feeling of going back to childhood yourself?

CHRIS Yes. You tend to remember the super good times, and then those mini-disasters, too.

DR. BRAZELTON What kind of disasters?

CHRIS Oh, I just think of the anticipation and disappointment: when my father was not on the 7:30 train from Boston, we knew he'd be off until the next night. I know Wiley will have to face this, but hopefully not too often.

DR. BRAZELTON How will you feel when you have to be away?

CHRIS I'll miss him.

DR. BRAZELTON That seems to make you sad.

CHRIS Well, it's such a special time, I hate to miss a night.

DR. BRAZELTON Is it just that you'll miss Wiley, or is it something more than that?

CHRIS Maybe more than that.

DR. BRAZELTON Are you afraid you're going to become too much like your own father?

CHRIS *Very quietly.* Mmmmm.

DR. BRAZELTON Not many people in your father's generation, you know, were open about how they felt. I suspect that the more important you were to him, the harder it was for him to show it. You

The Involved Father

know, seeing you with Wiley reminds me of how I *wanted* to be when my son was young. But, you know, it was *hard*. I saw myself falling back on the kind of relationship I had with my father, which was very distant. He was a great athlete and a great performer, but he never let me get very close, and I repeated that with my kids. But here you are, having changed jobs to get things organized the way you want them. You and Wiley will always have this time to look back on.

CHRIS   I hope so.

DR. BRAZELTON   If you let it get to you, you'll get back in that old mentality of either/or that you had with your own father. It doesn't need to be that way, you know. If you can save some time for him when you get home, and save enough energy, he'll build on what you already have together from this time early in his life.

THE ISSUES

Two strong forces are at work as Chris finds his way as a father: his memory of missing his own father, and the fact that Wiley was such a special baby, longed for over many years. When he and Robin finally adopted Wiley, Chris fell in love. He was ready for this little boy. Fortunately, Wiley is such a sensitive, adaptable fellow that he made fathering very rewarding for Chris. He not only looks like him – blond, strong, and well built – but his personality is already similar. Both reach out with a winning smile and charming eagerness. The only thing that Wiley hasn't got is the dimple in Chris's chin and his gold-rimmed glasses. Otherwise,

The Cutler Family

they are virtual replicas of each other. Chris and Wiley both look others over with a slightly cocked head and probing expression. They are absorbed in what they hear. Then, as if it were the most wonderful revelation, their faces brighten in understanding. Many of the mannerisms I noticed in these two are unique ones, so Wiley must have mimicked them from Chris. How could he have learned them so early? My only assumption is that, because Chris has been so available to this little boy, so devoted to his care, Wiley has had a constant opportunity to imitate, to absorb his father's behavior.

Chris's relationship with Wiley was of course fueled by the special circumstances of his adoption. Even on the trip home from South Carolina, Chris remembers himself as overwhelmed and captured. With such intense feelings mobilized from the start, it was easy for Chris to stay involved with this little boy. Each new achievement — smiling, vocalizing, laughing, reaching, sitting, walking — has become Chris's as well as Wiley's. He has relived his own infancy in this baby. They are locked in what psychoanalyst Margaret Mahler called a symbiotic relationship.

Wiley has kept up his end in building this bond. So far, he worships and rewards Chris daily. What will happen when Wiley becomes negative and resistant? Will Chris be able to understand this budding independence and participate in it with both admiration and patience? Will he see the second year as "terrific" or "terrible"? The rewards of fathering have been extra important to Chris. His close involvement with Wiley has brought him a deep satisfaction that will no doubt help him tolerate any future uncertainty, as well as the pull between his career and fatherhood.

Can a man and a woman really share equally in the job of child rearing? Diane Ehrensaft, in *Parenting Together*,* shows that wives are as influential in making this happen as are husbands. The women's movement has opened doors for all of us — women and men alike. As it helped women to assume, and then prove, that they could succeed in the workplace, the movement raised the next question: can men take on nurturing roles and will women let them? A few men have dared to test themselves. It takes a pretty

* New York: Free Press, 1987.

The Involved Father

strong ego, like Chris's, to modify the traditional masculine role. An involved father must face his male colleagues, who may be threatened by his choice and may jealously taunt him. Robin's ability to support the family through her successful interior design business, if she so chose, is another potential threat to Chris's image of his maleness.

Robin's image of herself as a nurturing woman is also at stake. Can she accept her dual role for long? In order to make it work, they both have to be committed to the conviction that their choices are good for Wiley. Fortunately, both Chris and Robin see that they are making a gift to Wiley. And Wiley has contributed his part. He literally sopped up his father. He reflected back his gestures, his expressions, his rhythms with such engaging charm that Chris couldn't help but be involved. Had Wiley been a girl, or a different personality, would Chris have remained so committed? We'll never know.

Is the new trend toward parenting together a revolution, or is it driven by necessity? Diane Ehrensaft says it is both. It is certainly changing strongly held cultural beliefs and practices, freeing women's ambitions and men's nurturing power. But shared parenting is also reinforced by necessity – the plight of nuclear families under financial stress and with no societal support for child care. Men are needed at home now. If children are not to be neglected, both parents must take an active role in child rearing. Not only do children benefit when fathers become more involved, but the family as a whole is strengthened. Perhaps, in the long run, the involvement of fathers can help reverse the devastating trend toward more and more family breakup. In my mind, there is no substitute for a stable family. The opportunity for small children to experience two deeply involved parents is a pediatrician's dream.

Over the years I've been in practice, I've watched the development of father-infant relationships. Public permission for fathers to become more involved first came in the 1960s from the childbirth education groups. Fathers were encouraged to attend childbirth classes and be present at delivery. Earlier, in the 1950s, a few men fought to be with their wives through labor and delivery. I tried with my first child, but allowed myself to be sent home toward the end of my wife's labor. There was still an aura of secrecy about delivery and little support for fathers to share the experience. Back at home, I felt a mixture of guilt at having brought my wife into this dangerous state, and also sadness at missing out on a glorious high – the birth of our first child. In retrospect, I think men were shut out of the delivery room because medical personnel felt their alert observation as competition, and hence dangerous. Also, fathers allowed themselves to be shut out because they accepted the notion that they didn't belong in this female rite of passage.

After Lamaze, Grantly Dick Read, and others changed labor into a participant affair in which women were alert and active, rather than medicated into passivity, the need for support during labor and delivery became clear. The role of grandmothers and other female relatives over the centuries was reaffirmed. More recently, Marshall Klaus and John Kennell demonstrated that when a *doula* (a Greek name for a woman who supports another in labor) is present, labor is shorter and there are less complications, including cesarean sections.* There is also less need for episiotomy, less tearing of the cervix, and less danger of complications for the fetus. In other words, support for a laboring woman makes the entire process more effective and safer. Both mother and baby profit. But grandmothers are not always available in this generation, and busy nurses must care for more than one laboring woman. The more that pregnant women began to recognize their need for a constant supportive person, the more evident it became that fathers were needed. Childbirth education courses came to be designed for both mothers and fathers. Women changed the course of fatherhood.

When a father is present at birth, his involvement with the baby immediately intensifies. His participation and handling of the newborn captures the father at a deep and lasting level. This effect, coupled with the fact that the majority of mothers now work, has led men increasingly to share responsibility for their children. I have seen the change gradually in my own practice. When they accompany their wives for a prenatal visit, they now bring as many questions as do their wives. They call me at my call hours. For many well-baby visits, fathers alone bring in the child. For most of the rest, both parents are present. When women are willing to share this nurturing responsibility, men respond.

---

* *New England Journal of Medicine*, 303:597–600 (September 11, 1980).

The Involved Father

Mothers benefit from a father's participation in more than practical ways. A decade ago, an important study* showed that mothers are more competent in feeding and playing with their four-week-old infants when the father is more supportive of them. The reverse is true; marital discord in this critical period is associated with inept mothering. The father's presence and support has been shown repeatedly to affect the kind of mothering a woman can muster.

In our research at Boston Children's Hospital, we have found that feelings of preoccupation, absorption, and interest in the baby can be generated by helping fathers understand the behavior of their newborn babies. When our Neonatal Behavioral Assessment Scale is demonstrated to fathers on the third day, these same fathers are significantly more sensitive to their babies' cries one month later and more involved not only with the baby but with the whole family one year later.† Fathers are there to be captured.

This involvement changes fathers as well as being good for their babies. Fathers develop new images of themselves as they seek and find the rewards of nurturing their own small babies. Of the young fathers I know in Cambridge, I can tell which ones are intimately involved with their children when I pass them on the street. They seem to walk taller; they look brighter and more confident. And of course they also tend to stop me on the street to tell me about any new step their baby has taken.

How competent are fathers? Ross Parke and his colleagues have shown that fathers fed their babies as successfully as did the mothers and were as sensitive to their small babies' cues.†† They feel that fathers would feed their babies more often if there were a shared perception in society that fathers were indeed as competent in caring for their infants as are mothers. The "maternal instinct"

---

* F. A. Pedersen, B. Anderson, and R. L. Cain, "An Approach to Understanding Linkage between the Parent-Infant and Spouse Relationship" (Paper presented at Society for Research in Child Development, New Orleans, March, 1977).

† J. Beal, "The Effect of Demonstration of the Neonatal Behavioral Assessment Scale on the Father/Infant Relationship," *Birth* (March 1989).

†† R. Parke, *Fathers*, Cambridge, Mass.: Harvard University Press, 1981.

The Cutler Family

has been assigned to mothers, and it will take a real change in society's attitudes before fathers feel skillful in this respect. If Robin, for instance, had criticized Chris in the early weeks for the way he held the baby or for being rough or clumsy, Chris would have been all too vulnerable. He would have been likely to pull back and to return these tasks to her. A new mother who needs her husband's involvement had better hold back her criticism of her husband's care of the baby in the first weeks. Even pediatricians are highly sensitive to their wives' criticism as they handle their first baby. Women start off with nine months' experience of the newborn as well as more positive expectations from others. Men must learn confidence. In Robin and Chris's case, the event of adoption may have helped pave the way to their shared roles. They both started from the same point. Robin did not have the head start of pregnancy. Both were starved for this boy. Both were ready to share and to develop their relationship around him.

What does the baby gain from a father's involvement? The opportunity for babies to learn about two different caregivers who are committed to them is a real investment in the future. At our Child Development Unit at Boston Children's Hospital, my colleagues Suzanne Dixon and Michael Yogman and I observed films of four- to six-week-old babies sitting in infant seats as they interacted with adults who were off-camera.* We watched the babies' fingers, toes, facial movements, eyes, and mouth for two minutes without seeing with whom they were interacting. After two minutes, we could successfully identify whether a baby was interacting with a mother, father, or stranger by the way his or her body behaved. Our observations demonstrated that with mothers, babies have already developed an expectancy for a low-key, gentle interaction. Their fingers, toes, eyes, and mouth move more rhythmically – reaching out, curling up, opening, closing in a smooth rhythm four times a minute. For when mothers play with their babies, they invariably lean over them, containing them with hands, voice, and face, encouraging a smooth duet which matches the babies' own slow, smooth rhythms. Fathers never are smooth. By

---

* S. Dixon et al., "Early Social Interaction of Infants with Parents and Strangers," *Journal of the American Academy of Child Psychiatry* (1981).

the time the baby is four to six weeks old, when the father has been involved, a baby's shoulders, face, eyebrows, mouth, arms, even feet, go up when a father enters the scene, in what we call a "pounce" look. The babies look as though they expected to be pounced upon.

Fathers, despite their increasing participation in everyday care, still expect to spend a larger percentage of their time in play with their babies. In an earlier book, *On Becoming a Family*, I describe this jazzing-up approach which fathers take, even in the beginning. They engage in more physical games, such as bouncing and lifting, than do mothers. Mothers' activity revolves more around feeding, teaching, and demonstrating toys. By four to six weeks of age, these different expectations can be identified in a baby's filmed behavior.

Experience with two parents gives babies twice as rich a start, and more to learn. Their range of emotional development is enhanced. Psychologist Tiffany Field has shown that "primary caretaking" fathers smile and imitate their babies' facial expressions and vocalizations more than fathers who are "secondary caretakers."* Wiley's opportunity to develop different ways of reacting to his world is certainly enhanced by Chris's deep involvement.

Even in the newborn period, fathers react differentially to sons and daughters. They touch and talk most with boys. Mothers talk to and touch their daughters more than their sons. Such differences continue. Ross Parke and Douglas Sawin, prominent investigators of newborn behavior, found that fathers touch and play with sons more but showed more quick affection for daughters, while mothers continue to touch and talk more to daughters and to hold their sons close.† In these observations we may see the earliest evidence for sex role typing. In my experience, however, newborn babies contribute actively to these differences in the way parents react to them. If, as with Wiley, a boy is quietly observant and responsive to quiet, gentle handling, both mother and father are likely to pick up these behavioral patterns and to fit in with them.

---

* T. Field, "Interaction Behaviors of Primary vs. Secondary Caretaker Fathers," *Developmental Psychology* 14 (1978).

† R. Parke and D. Sawin, "The Family in Early Infancy," in Pederson (ed.), *The Father-Infant Relationship*, New York: Praeger, 1980.

Chris and Wiley showed me the kind of relationship that is possible when a father is truly involved. Each seemed to be picking up the other's nonverbal cues without even looking directly at him; when Wiley moved, Chris moved almost imperceptibly in response. Before Chris gave him a direction, Wiley had started to carry it out. Such communication is based on a high degree of sensory communication. These two were not particularly active or boisterous. Their motor responses were precisely synchronized. To me, this represents not only the amount of effort and direct involvement that Chris brought to his role, but also the quality of their relationship. They were deeply in tune with each other.

A boy's intellectual development is more dependent on father's presence than is a girl's. Boys who have more frequent contact with their fathers score higher on cognitive measures. Fathers not only stimulate the son's development of physical prowess but also directly increase cognitive performance. Fathers of girls stimulate cognitive processes more indirectly through verbal praise and compliments. These positive effects are seen in tests as early as age six months and as late as six to seven years as children enter school. The reverse is also true. A father's absence affects achievement test scores, IQ scores, and grade point average.* A father's involvement in child rearing does not seem to alter sex role identifications, except in regard to housework. When fathers take part in the day-to-day chores of the household, both boys and girls are more familiar with all these chores. Boys like Wiley, whose fathers are involved, will be better fitted to adjust to the pressures and tasks facing the ever-increasing numbers of two-career families.

COMMON QUESTIONS

QUESTION   I've had a difficult time reconciling the demands of my job with the time I want to spend

---

* M. Shinn, "Father Absence and Cognitive Development," *Psychological Bulletin*, 85 (1978) 295.

with my son at home. Have you any suggestions?

DR. BRAZELTON Save up enough energy during the day so you can go home to gather him up and get close to him. Share a bit of time with him when you first get home – and listen to him. It's not so much the length of time that matters as long as there is some *every* day. Then on weekends have a special time that is sacred with just you and him. Do what *he* wants then. Talk about your special time all the rest of the week. The special quality of this shared time will keep your relationship alive and important.

QUESTION When my children were growing up, I changed an enormous number of diapers, and I was very good at burping and all that stuff. But it was a chore and I was not particularly glad about doing it. I was really worried about my career and whether I'd make it; I thought the kids would grow up anyway. Now I wonder if they would have grown up more secure if had they felt more joy from me.

DR. BRAZELTON I'm sure that it meant a great deal to your children that you got your hands dirty. Children won't just grow up anyway. What I hear is your own longing, wishing you'd been even more involved. But it sounds as though they got a lot of you at a good time.

QUESTION I grew up in a fairly traditional home. My mother was a full-time mother; my dad worked. My wife works, so I care for our child quite a bit, changing and bathing, etc. Is it normal for fathers in my position to feel that they're doing more but that other fathers are not?

DR. BRAZELTON Yes. This is all part of meeting the demands of a new, unfamiliar role. I'm sure that many fathers today feel they are doing "everything," and no one really cares. Working women have always felt that. But the truth is, these ordinary, caring chores are important, to you as well as to your children. When they don't need you any longer, you'll be surprised to feel a gap in your life. But now it is placing unfamiliar demands on you, and it is normal to feel resentful. Just don't let yourself act on it. You are giving your children a chance to experience how nurturant a father can be. They'll be better at it when their time comes.

QUESTION I watch my daughter Hannah full time, and I think I have a great advantage of being able to see subtle changes as they take place. It's an amazing time. Sometimes men will see me and say, "Giving the wife a little break?" I explain that I take care of her full time and what a joy it is, but they don't seem interested.

DR. BRAZELTON They probably don't want to hear you. Most men today are aware that they're missing something if they don't participate fully. These developmental changes that you see and feel responsible for can make you want more. I hope you can see it in her face, too, that look of "I just did it myself." That's the most important thing you can give her — a sense of herself!

QUESTION We're going through the planning stages. My wife and I both have strenuous careers. Even

The Involved Father

though I've worked hard for this, I think a baby might become the most important thing to me. I'd probably sacrifice a promotion for my child. How can we plan for this? It's such a personal decision.

DR. BRAZELTON And it's a major one. No matter how much planning you do in advance, it will be more demanding and more exciting than you can imagine. All I can say is leave your options open. In my book *Working and Caring*, I try to give an honest picture of what mothering and fathering is like when both parents work.

QUESTION What would you say to a mother feeling her territory is being invaded by a father wanting to take a stronger role, such as a father wanting to do it all his way – the diapering or the washing of the clothes or how to play with the child? My husband and I do things differently, and I feel threatened when he just takes over with our son.

DR. BRAZELTON You had better talk it out, the sooner the better. Many mothers experience these unconscious feelings of competition for the important nurturing role. But there is room for both parents. The more each of you gives the child, the better it will be for him, *as long as* it doesn't cause irreparable friction between the parents. Do everything you can to guard against this and to understand the source of friction. It comes from caring so much. That's a real plus for the child – to have you both care. Don't ruin it!

The Cutler Family

Parental Rivalry

ॐ

OFFICE VISIT

Robin and Chris brought Wiley to my office at the age of eighteen months. They sat close to each other; Chris pulled the "father's chair" up to my desk, next to the chair Robin had chosen. As he sat down, I noticed that she leaned toward him. Wiley stood at his mother's knee, holding on to her with one hand, but watching his father.

DR. BRAZELTON I'm glad to see the three of you. Let's see now, how old is Wiley?

ROBIN Wiley is one and a half going on four, sometimes. He really wants control. He's being assertive and independent and noisy, rambunctious – is it because he's a boy? I sort of get wistful and sad about that, when I think about his growing up and going away. He's been so good up to now.

DR. BRAZELTON How is it difficult now?

ROBIN Well, for one thing, he seems to want to do more for his dad than he does for his mom!

DR. BRAZELTON That's not very fair or easy for you, is it?

ROBIN Some days, no, it isn't. With Chris at work, I get all the no's during the day, and when Chris comes home, Wiley slips into a happy, playful, I'll-do-anything-to-be-with-my-dad mood.

DR. BRAZELTON	Makes you feel like you're doing all the hard work, and he gets all the gravy.
ROBIN	Exactly.
DR. BRAZELTON	Maybe a little competition comes into this.
ROBIN	Quite a lot some days!
DR. BRAZELTON	Does this make for stress between the two of you?
ROBIN	Yes, it can.
DR. BRAZELTON	Chris, can we get a urine sample from Wiley? *With Chris out of the room, maybe she can open up.*
CHRIS	Say goodbye for a minute. Say goodbye to Mom.
WILEY	'Bye.
DR. BRAZELTON	You're the best boy! *To Robin.* The trouble with the second year is that you have to give up the love affair of the first year. There's really nothing that you can depend on anymore. He's unpredictable now – for his own reasons, not yours. He doesn't just worship you.
ROBIN	*Sounding sad.* So true.
DR. BRAZELTON	In the first year, everything you do with a baby comes right back to you. Is it just the opposite now?
ROBIN	It's not total rejection, but I have feelings of that.

The Cutler Family

DR. BRAZELTON   Does Chris feel this? I wouldn't have known this from anything he's said.

ROBIN   He doesn't see it like I do. For instance, the other day I was in the kitchen trying to prepare dinner, and Wiley wanted to help out. He kept trying to reach up and put his hand on the burners. I had to stop him. Then he started screaming, "Daddy, Daddy, Daddy!" And I found myself getting so upset, because I was trying to handle the situation and Chris comes in and starts telling me what to do. I held on to Wiley even tighter saying, "I can handle it, I can handle it, I'm the mommy, you know," and he's still screaming for his daddy.

DR. BRAZELTON   What do you think is happening?

ROBIN   He's a very involved father –

DR. BRAZELTON   Very.

ROBIN   – which . . . well, I wouldn't want it any other way. I do mean that, even though we have these moments of competition.

Clearly, Robin understood her conflict, but she still couldn't help how she felt. As Wiley and Chris returned, Wiley ignored her; she tried to hold on, first with her eyes and then by reaching for him. Chris led Wiley to her, but Robin's look said it all. She was still hurting. I decided to try something different.

DR. BRAZELTON   You know, this fellow is a real showman. He really knows how to win people over. I can feel it. He not only wants to be like the men in his life, but he also wants to win us over to his side.

Parental Rivalry

ROBIN   Is that something that happens – the gender
                   identification, I think people call it? *Her ques-*
                   tion was my answer.

DR. BRAZELTON   Why do you ask that?

ROBIN   I don't know. Maybe I don't want a chauvinist
                   on my hands . . .

DR. BRAZELTON   Like his daddy?

ROBIN   That's not what I meant! *She was really asking*
                   something deeper.

DR. BRAZELTON   What is it you're longing for?

ROBIN   With Wiley, you mean?

DR. BRAZELTON   Well, is there something else?

ROBIN   Actually, I'd love a daughter, too.

DR. BRAZELTON   Somebody like you?

ROBIN   Somebody like me. Sure. That's a real fantasy
                   of mine.

DR. BRAZELTON   It's interesting that Chris doesn't feel as com-
                   petitive for Wiley with you, as you do with
                   him. So you think it might have to do with
                   the fact that they're both male?

ROBIN   Probably.

DR. BRAZELTON   Do you feel that there's a lot going on there
                   that you haven't any part of?

The Cutler Family

ROBIN　　　　　　　Yes. I mean, he's identifying with his dad, and that's two against one. *Such a natural feeling.*

CHRIS　　　　　　　Maybe I'll end up like that, if we have a little daughter.

DR. BRAZELTON　There's no "maybe" about it; you'll end up like that! Jealous! *To both.* But can you also see how good this is? You care so much that you want to scrabble for him – it's very nice for *him.* It may not be easy for you and your relationship, but it's an inevitable part of a triangle – tensions and excitement and frustration and affection. Your involvement is great for him.

ROBIN　　　　　　　So you feel he's OK?

DR. BRAZELTON　Not just OK, he's *great*! How about you?

ROBIN　　　　　　　I'll be all right.

DR. BRAZELTON　I think you will.

THE ISSUES

The kind of jealousy that Robin feels is a natural sequel to the intensity of Chris and Wiley's relationship. She is likely to feel left out as they grow closer and more alike. As men become more involved in their families, such feelings are bound to surface more and more. It is inevitable that adults who care will be in competition for a child. In the past, this kind of competition has even motivated caring nurses and doctors to keep parents out of children's hospitals. Unconsciously, they said to themselves, "I can do better by this sick child." As fathers become more nurturing, mothers will feel somewhat supplanted. Sharing parents need to be aware

Parental Rivalry

that these feelings are healthy, in order to avoid endangering their relationship. Men who assume that women have more nurturing instincts are likely to overreact. I remember asking my wife if she was sure she had enough breast milk – a question I would *never* have asked a patient. In retrospect, I realize I was intensely jealous of her and of the baby. In these and more subtle ways, men will try to shove mothers aside. To protect themselves, women are likely to criticize their husbands. Neither of these reactions is necessary, if competitive feelings are understood. Instead, jealousy can be a motivating force, energizing both parents to reach out to the child. It needn't be destructive. The baby can profit by this heightened passion.

Diane Ehrensaft, in her book mentioned earlier, points out interesting differences in the way parents behave with the same child. Mothers commented on the clashing outfits that their husbands chose when they dressed the children. They were more likely to match colors and took more pride in how their children looked. Men, in turn, were scornful of their wives' attention to appearance. Each was expressing a measure of competition in a rather safe, noncritical area.

Worrying is another arena in which parents are likely to differ – and to compete. Mothers are more likely to worry in advance. Men worry after something has already happened. Mothers tend to feel that they are more closely in tune with children's oncoming adjustments. Men only identify when they can see something happen. Men are more likely to say, "At work, I have to forget about what's happening at home. If I worry too much about the kids, I can't do my work well." If there is indeed such a sex difference in the way parents focus their concern, this could benefit children. They could turn to mothers to prepare for a big adjustment, to fathers for support as they make the adjustment. Each parent can serve a different supportive role, whereas the same sort of worrying from both parents might well overload a child with concern.

I have long been fascinated by how early a child recognizes the difference in his parents and plays on it. During the first year, our children "knew" their mother worried about feeding, so they saved their problems with meals for her. They ate fine for me. In the toilet training area in the second year, it was just the reverse. My wife had utter faith in their ultimate success in this area. So the children tortured me with their "mistakes." When one parent's tension around an issue is balanced by a more relaxed attitude on the part of the other, the child is cushioned against an obsessive overconcern. By the same token, when both parents are uptight about any one issue, it is more likely that the child *will* develop a problem in that specific area.

As Wiley declares his independence in the second year, Chris and Robin are likely to experience it very differently. Robin feels it deeply as a loss of the "love affair" of a baby's first year. Chris feels it as a kind of blossoming of Wiley's masculinity. As the separation progresses, however, Chris may reexperience the memories of his own father – with whom the alternating closeness and separation was so painful. Now that Wiley has begun to establish his own identity separate from his father's, will Chris be able to let him go? I felt that he was already hanging on to Wiley in a pretty intense fashion. Maybe Robin senses this hanging on and feels even more shut out as a result.

It is no coincidence that parental rivalry surfaces at this period in a toddler's development. The child's struggle for autonomy kindles its intensity. An increased dependence is seen in all toddlers just before they start to break away in the second year. They cry when you turn your back to walk away, they wake more often at night, they cling in any new situation. Within a month or two, they are ready to take off without so much as a backward look. But in the meanwhile, their inner struggles make them provoking and difficult, even to the point of tantrums. Sensing rivalry between their parents, toddlers may draw them into the struggle. The parents' task is to see all this as the child's issue, not theirs.

The competitive feelings, the jealousy which each parent is liable to feel at such a period of intense adjustment, serves a purpose however. As a toddler clings to one, then the other parent, the rejected parent is learning to let go. Wiley will soon begin to ignore Chris and cling to Robin. His attachments will continue to alternate. This is the way Wiley and his parents will learn the pain and passion of separation.

Parental Rivalry

COMMON QUESTIONS

QUESTION   Why do children cling to one parent at one time and another parent at another time?

DR. BRAZELTON They are identifying with one parent so passionately that they need to exclude the other. Later, they'll turn all their attention on the other parent and exclude the first.

QUESTION   In a family with a nurturing father and a working mother, are the sexual identities of the children affected?

DR. BRAZELTON I would expect children from such families to have wider options: a working and nurturing role model for both males and females. If they can see that men and women can be effective in both roles, they will be fortunate children indeed.

QUESTION   We have a problem among ourselves in terms of the way we care for our daughter. I do things when I'm tending her which are totally different from what my wife does with her. For instance, I think we should let our daughter cry herself to sleep, but my wife finds this hard. How can we deal with this? And what effect will it have on our daughter?

DR. BRAZELTON These differences are common. Try not to argue over them. The tension between you is what could be damaging. Each of you can deal entirely differently with your daughter, and she'll manage to know what to expect from each of you. As long as she knows you care

The Cutler Family

and aren't full of conflict, a child can sort out two different sets of behavior and expectations. As for the sleep issue, have a look at the discussion of sleep in *To Listen to a Child*. Perhaps the two of you could agree about when to go in and when not to. If not, let one of you take charge each night.

QUESTION   My husband and I have the same problem. I feel that our baby is my job during the day, and when my husband comes home and starts taking care of him, I'm almost afraid he's going to do a better job. So, in order to keep the edge, I tend to try to correct him on how to put the diaper on, or what to feed her. My husband always gets compliments on what a good daddy he is. Mothers never get compliments. We're expected to do it.

DR. BRAZELTON   If you want him to stay involved, don't look over his shoulder. It may be unfair, but for the present, mothers are expected to be responsible and fathers are seen as supplemental. Children sense this, and usually turn to their mother first and to father only as a backup. The rewards of being the responsible one balance things out.

QUESTION   Was there less rivalry between spouses in your generation compared to ours, now that the father is participating more?

DR. BRAZELTON   The rivalries we felt were never openly expressed and were more destructive as a result. Most of us allowed ourselves to be kept out of a very important role with our children. I'd have liked to be much more involved, but, even as a pediatrician, I was too unsure and felt that it was a woman's job and women were better at it. Don't let that happen to you. Of course, rivalry will be part of shared parenting, but these days you can address it more openly. It generates a lot of energy to offer to the baby, who can really profit from it.

QUESTION   Sometimes my husband and I use the children to get at each other, and I wonder how we can stop doing that.

DR. BRAZELTON   You are right to be concerned. To use children this way can scare them. I would suggest that you air your differences openly without the children present. You don't need to agree on how you deal with the children, but you do need to back each other up.

QUESTION   Once you've figured out how to spend enough time alone with each child, when do you fit in spending time as a family and spending time as husband and wife?

DR. BRAZELTON   Maybe you have to schedule each of those. Now that there are so many two-parent working families, the pressures on time are enormous. Just set it up so that each of these important relationships in your life has some time each week. Hire a sitter or whatever you need. It's an investment for the future.

QUESTION   I still don't see how rivalry can be positive for a child.

The Cutler Family

DR. BRAZELTON   It can be, if it's understood and doesn't become destructive. Rivalry mobilizes energy and shows that the child is top priority for both of you. A child growing up with that knowledge is bound to feel secure.

Grandparenting

⤞

OFFICE VISIT

Robin and Chris were going away on a vacation together, and Robin's mother, "Bommer," was going to babysit. She came in with Robin before they left. Robin was feeling the usual qualms about leaving her toddler. And yet it was obvious to me that Wiley and his grandmother are very close.

DR. BRAZELTON Robin, he's pushing you today, isn't he?

Robin nodded. Wiley was clearly teasing to see how far he could go, alternately cuddling and pulling away from Robin. As we talked about her trip, he climbed on her lap, ignoring his grandmother's smiles.

DR. BRAZELTON He certainly wants to hang on to you before you go.

At this point, Bommer spoke coaxingly to Wiley about a walk on the beach.

BOMMER   Do you remember how you came to visit me on Cape Cod and we went for a walk to watch the seagulls?

As Bommer described the gulls, her arms and her hands mimicked the gulls so beautifully that we were all mesmerized. Wiley drew closer to her involuntarily. Looking at him, she described how the waves broke on the shore, sending up spray in beautiful swoops very much like the seagulls. Wiley watched her gestures with awe and wonder in his eyes.

The Cutler Family

BOMMER   Maybe you and I could sit together on one of those seagulls' backs and swoop and swoop and swoop. We'd watch the gull soar over the water, then over the land, and we'd sit very close – like this.

By now, Wiley was huddled up next to her, his body pressing into hers, his eyes dreaming – as if in some faraway land.

DR. BRAZELTON   What do you worry about when you take care of your grandson?

BOMMER   Well, I hope there won't be any problems or accidents.

DR. BRAZELTON   Are you worried about disciplining somebody else's child?

BOMMER   Oh, very. I don't want to be reprimanded myself. *So typical. Grandmothers are often afraid they will be judged.*

DR. BRAZELTON   I guess it's really important that you all prepare Wiley for separation. *To Bommer.* You needn't feel so guilty when he's cranky and upset and not very interested in you. That's bound to happen. Today I think the fact that he'll talk to you at all is really very sweet. *To Robin.* The main thing is to tell him that even if you go away, you're going to be back.

Robin appeared to be listening, but was looking at the two others at the same time. As soon as I spoke to Bommer, she picked Wiley up herself. Separation will be hard on Robin, too.

DR. BRAZELTON   Does he remind you at all of Robin when she was two?

Grandparenting

BOMMER	Oh, yes. A great deal. She was very independent.
DR. BRAZELTON	You say that with a certain edge to your voice.
BOMMER	Well, it was hard to keep track of her, and a lot of work. I feel that I have to watch him very carefully, too, you see.
DR. BRAZELTON	Is there a little controlling in this?
BOMMER	Well . . . *She pauses.*
DR. BRAZELTON	There's no need to apologize; I just want to understand what you were saying.
BOMMER	I think that's true.
DR. BRAZELTON	Do you still feel that way?
BOMMER	*Laughing.* Yes, definitely. In certain situations. *She looks at Robin.*
ROBIN	I get that message: mother knows best. And she does, sometimes. And yet, I want to do it *my* way. It's my child, my turn.

Mother and daughter were exploring new ground. They needed reassurance, and Wiley would help.

ROBIN	I feel like I'm five years old again as I talk this way. It takes me right back to being a child who has to have permission from mother. *A mother, but still very much a daughter.*
DR. BRAZELTON	Does it bother you that she feels controlled?

The Cutler Family

BOMMER   I don't *want* her to feel that way. Anyway, I think that as she raises Wiley, I will fade from the picture. *A grandmother, yearning for involvement but very cautious.*

ROBIN   I don't think that your influence will diminish *ever.*

BOMMER   Thank you.

ROBIN   Our *relationship* is the basis for so many things, particularly where mothering is concerned.

DR. BRAZELTON   And yet you sound like you're apologizing for feeling critical.

ROBIN   I do apologize, sometimes. Well, yes –

DR. BRAZELTON   Isn't it all right to feel critical?

ROBIN   Yes, but ... *Both mother and daughter feel afraid to criticize, without knowing why.* Actually, you know, why aren't *I* standing up for *Robin* and saying, "*I'm* in charge?"

DR. BRAZELTON   Why aren't you?

ROBIN   *Laughing.* Come on, Mother. Why?

This mother-daughter story was a natural one, even necessary, if their relationship was to grow.

DR. BRAZELTON   This reticence is a very basic part of your relationship, and yet you both seem aware of what is going on. What *both* of you are sensing is how much you need each other. But that makes you, Robin, yearn to be five years old again. That's normal. But you've got to stand up for your grown-up side as well. It's a big struggle. *To Bommer.* She really does need you at a time like this.

BOMMER   It's a new fulfillment for her, and that I appreciate.

DR. BRAZELTON   And I can see where she gets all her lovely nurturance.

BOMMER   It's a hand-me-down.

DR. BRAZELTON   Wonderful, isn't it?

THE ISSUES

A grandparent serves many purposes for a child, which no parent can fulfill. And yet, as we see in Robin, jealous feelings are bound to arise when a parent watches her child in the thrall of her own parent. The threat of becoming dependent again, the pain of sharing a child's affections, are experienced very deeply. Of course, this is balanced by warm feelings of security and relief. Knowing a grandparent is there for backup is comforting. We have taken over on weekends sometimes for our daughter with her baby, just so that she and her husband could sleep solidly for eighteen hours. Although in their sleep-deprived state it was lifesaving, they still questioned what went on: "Did he miss me? Did you change him as soon as he needed it? Did you put him down for his nap on time? How much did he eat – for you?" Through these questions they maintained a sense of continuity with their baby. Behind these questions was the same kind of competition that we've seen Robin and Bommer experiencing. A grandparent is bound to endanger a parent's sense of her own competence. The better the grandparent was as a parent, the greater the threat.

The Cutler Family

When I ask parents-to-be whether they will have their parents to help with the new baby, some say, "Never." When I ask them why, they reply, "They'd tell us what to do. And we want to do it our own way." Sometimes I point out that if the grandparents say, "This is the way to do it," and they reply, "I'd *never* do it that way," they have helped themselves clarify their own path. At the same time, however, I support their decision. They do need to find out their own way and at their own speed. In such a situation, a sensitive grandparent will say, "I'll come later when they need me – when they've found their own way, made their own mistakes. I don't want to meddle. I want them to find their own answers." It is rare these days for young couples to see their parents as a mirror into the past and toward the future, as representing experience and a repository of cultural values. In our nuclear family culture, each new generation searches for its *own* values, even if it is a lonely search. Without the last generation as a backup, young families can feel anxious and anchorless.

Now that both parents work in most families, the need for help from grandparents is more urgent than ever. But grandparents have their own lives, and usually both are working, too. The same parent who wants to find her own way may come to say, "I wish my mother were nearby so I could leave my baby with her." When there is a lot of distance between the generations, the image of the helpful grandparent can become romanticized. Leaving a baby with any close relative can create tensions unless all members of the family work to avoid them. Sharing a baby with an outsider, curiously enough, is somewhat easier to handle. With a grandparent, parents are more apt to wonder, "Does she love Grandma more than me if I'm away all day?" A parent's own unresolved struggles can interfere with his or her feeling of self-assurance, as they did for Robin.

But grandparents offer so much. They are outside the immediate Oedipal struggle and bring perspective to intimate family dramas. They need not be as authoritarian as parents. They can be indulgent without worrying about precedents which must be broken later. They can be permissive and relaxed, while parents must worry about family schedules and discipline. No wonder a parent feels jealous! The generations had better agree on some ground rules.

Grandparents show children the mountaintops, while parents must teach the drudgeries of how to get there. My own grandmother was a magical figure for me. She used to tell me stories which became part of my dreams. I wanted to please her so much that when she said, "Berry's so good with babies," she opened the door to my present profession. I kept wanting to please her and still hear her today whenever anyone says, "You're so good with babies." I hope she hears it, too. Of course, my mother was jealous of my grandmother, but she was wrong. I needed them both – but for different things.

A grandparent like Bommer can provide a whole new source of experiences. She can enjoy Wiley's negativism; she can see the value of his spirit. If she can keep her critical feelings out of the way, and avoid saying to Robin, "If you'd only do such and such, he wouldn't be like that," she can bring a nonjudgmental perspective to the whole family. A grandparent should always try to turn the coin over, look for the other side of the developmental process in which the parent and child are struggling.

Grandparents can also convey what their family stands for by letting their grandchildren into their lives and past. Strong family values are passed on by example and identification. As humans, our long childhood provides us with the chance to learn about our culture and our families' values and to have the chance to incorporate them at our own speed, through trial and error. A long history of exposure to grandparents gives children a chance both to absorb and to test out the strengths, principles, and beliefs that characterize each family.

SUGGESTIONS FOR GRANDPARENTS

Many grandparents wonder how to make themselves important to their grandchildren and useful to their children, the parents. Here are good ways to begin:

The Cutler Family

FIRST OF ALL, STICK UP FOR YOUR UNIQUE ROLE. You are not the child's parent, and you don't need to be. If you can make your role one of approval, of loving delight in the child, and of reliable support for the parents, you will become important to both generations. It won't hurt to talk to the parents about limits for treats and indulgences. They may resent your being too generous and permissive. But they will certainly appreciate being cushioned themselves at times of stress.

OFFER TO SIT REGULARLY AND AT A TIME WHEN THEY NEED YOU. If you can babysit to avoid day care for small infants or after school care for older children, any working parent will be eternally grateful. If not, what about offering Saturday nights on a regular basis? Or have them all over to dinner on Sunday. I still remember Sundays at my in-laws' house, when our children were small, as an island in the midst of the chaos of our weekly lives. We groaned about getting up in time on Sunday morning, but we loved the sumptuous family feasts and the freedom of leaving the kids in the afternoon while we walked together on Boston Common.

PROVIDE THE FOCUS AND THE MEANS FOR HOLIDAY REUNIONS. Although everyone complains about the practical difficulties of getting together, there are few more meaningful ways for an extended family to keep in touch. Override all your children's objections and say, "We're having it, and we hope you'll come. We want you." Children always get sick at Christmas or at Easter. Reassure their parents: "Bring them and we'll nurse them." Parents always find it difficult to ask for leave at Chanukah. Remind them that holidays are for celebration. Try to emphasize the reunion and the fun and not the logistics. Some grandparents start worrying about the mechanics of holidays long before Thanksgiving. Of course, there will be stress for all three generations. Everyone will be fractious and will work off their tensions on each other. But the memories of the good moments will live on. We recently had twenty-four members of our extended family for Christmas dinner at our house. Both my wife and I were flattened by the experience.

But I know that it's things like this which my grandparents did for us that makes me remember my family as close and caring. I hope my children will do this for their children. My cousins and I still call on each other when we need to, because our grandparents set it up that way. We are an extended family, and we're all proud of it.

MAKE RITUALS OUT OF YOUR MEETINGS WITH YOUR GRANDCHILDREN. Take them an age-appropriate toy as a present, even if it's not Christmas or a birthday. Take them on an outing to a special museum or restaurant or park. Then be sure you have a time alone with each grandchild when you can talk or just be together. Most children love to hear about their own parents at their age. They like to hear about "the old days." This is your chance to give them a sense of family history. I've always made up rather fanciful stories for my children on long trips. For my grandchildren, I intend to make up stories about cowboys or survival days in Texas when I was a child their age. These will not necessarily be exactly true, but they won't be untrue and we'll all live in fantasy together.

DON'T TELL YOUR OWN CHILDREN WHAT TO DO — ESPECIALLY IN FRONT OF THE GRANDCHILDREN. The biggest danger is that you'll feel so strongly about your grandchildren that you'll feel you need to protect them. Undermining their parents in front of them is *never* good for children. It merely strengthens rebellion in the grandchildren and tends to set up tensions between parents and children. Of course, you will wish to make things perfect for your grandchildren. Probably the most sensitive areas will be those in which you feel you made a mistake with your own children and wish you could correct it. But you won't change anything by interference. If you feel strongly, take the parents aside and discuss the matter openly and calmly, listening to their point of view. But if you do this too much, or in a bossy way, you'll just strengthen your own children's feeling of insecurity as parents. They'll fight back and resent your intrusion. If you can be sup-

The Cutler Family

portive, you're much more likely to find they'll turn to you for advice.

OFFER BOTH GENERATIONS AN EMOTIONAL SANC-TUARY AND STABILITY. That means that you often have to keep your mouth shut even when it looks as if you could offer a simple solution. Grandparents no longer need to be parents, nor are they teachers. That's the lovely freedom of the role. Just sit and rock in the midst of chaos. Let them come to you. You can offer comfort, family love, experience, hugs, and a sense of strength and stability for each member of the family. Parents must be the disciplinarians. Teaching, in a direct sense, is better left to them and to teachers. You can offer children a sense of family customs and of wisdom *when* they ask for it. They will be learning from you whenever they are with you, but by example. Your grandchildren will learn more from modeling themselves on you than they will from any directions or advice you can offer them or their parents. Be the person you want them to remember.

DON'T RUSH UP TO SMALL CHILDREN, UNLESS YOU WANT THEM TO WITHDRAW. Looking small babies or children in the face when you first meet them is like an assault, and they will be bound to overreact. Never grab them out of their parents' arms – the safety of those arms is too critical. If you look just past them at their parents and wait for them to solicit you, they'll be yours before long. Their personal space is too precious. The more excited they are about your coming, the more they'll overreact by withdrawing when you finally arrive. I often carry a toy in my pocket. Then I look just beyond the small child, dangling the toy so they have to approach me to reach for it. As they come nearer, I let them realize that they have broken the safe boundary. I wait then until they look to me for approval about taking the toy. Then I speak gently to them – still not staring in their faces. It's all too easy to overload an excited, wary child. After I see their anxiety lessen, I know I can move in closer. Eventually, grandparents can be certain that their grandchildren will try for their attention. You have plenty of time.

KEEP INVOLVED WHEN YOU'RE FAR AWAY:

- Send postcards and pictures suited to the grandchild's age. Send a copy of a photo of the child's parent at the same age. This always fascinates a child.
- Birthday cards and birthday presents – especially ones you make – can become a symbol of grandparents.
- Use the telephone to say hello or offer congratulations on any small triumph.
- Videotapes are a new way to communicate. All children love to see someone they know on a TV screen.
- Make regular visits, but for short periods. Three days may be an optimal visit. If you stay longer, be sure you don't wear out your welcome. Pitch in and help with housework and with children. Try to take the family out to dinner or to the movies. Make a little party out of some moment of your visit.
- Keep in touch with each grandchild's particular joys and interests and encourage these with small offerings of stones, books, clippings or photographs, and timely congratulations.

COMMON QUESTIONS

QUESTION

My mother lives with us, so the problem of slipping back into a parent-child relationship is a constant concern. How can I let my children know I'm in charge without offending her?

DR. BRAZELTON

You are a fortunate three generations if you can do it without too much tension. I think your child does need to know you are the final authority, but that is hard to miss if you are the center of decision making as you should be. If this seems to bother your mother, you should talk it out away from the children.

The Cutler Family

QUESTION   What should I do when the whole family is sitting around together – all three generations – and one of the kids acts up and really makes a nuisance of herself? Should I correct her in front of my daughter or should I wait?

DR. BRAZELTON   As a grandparent, I would suggest that you sit back and leave it to the parents. If you do get into it, you will just unsettle them. Then they'll either overreact or underreact. If they don't, after it's over you might say to your daughter that when one of the kids acts up, she's in charge. Say that you don't want the children confused about this just because you are there.

QUESTION   How does a child reconcile his grandparents' permissiveness and indulgences and his parents' rules and limits?

DR. BRAZELTON   They know the difference very early. If neither generation is confused about its role with a child, he learns to behave appropriately with each one. When he tests you out, say to him, "You can do that with Grandma because she's a grandma. I'm your mommy and you know that you can't do it with me." This can be difficult, because a parent feels like such an ogre and wonders whether the child will resent her in contrast to his indulgent grandparent. Try to remember that discipline is a central part of parenting. Consistent limits are very reassuring to children, for a firm parent offers security.

QUESTION   I have a beautiful three-year-old granddaughter. She's been coming to my house almost every day, so I'm extremely close to her, especially since I've retired and have lots more time to play with her, read with her, and so on. But her mother's going to have a new baby. I'm wondering how I am ever going to have the same relationship with this new one as I have with the first one. I guess there must be one special grandchild, and the others you just love.

DR. BRAZELTON   What a beautiful grandparent statement. Of course, she'll always be *the* special one, and she'll know it. Isn't she lucky? She'll be shored up for the competition with her new sibling. You put in words what every parent also feels about a new baby: "How will I ever love her as much?" You will, but you'll love her differently. To have a grandparent who cares so much is like having a fortune in the bank.

QUESTION   What legacies can grandparents leave their grandchildren – other than money?

DR. BRAZELTON   The legacy of being loved unconditionally. Grandparents can afford to let the child test them, try things out on them that parents must nip in the bud. By listening and understanding them, you give them a sense that they are loved for their own sakes, not their accomplishments. Then, too, you hand on cultural and familial values which are more important than money.

QUESTION   On birthdays and holidays, we really want to be with our children. If we don't get an invitation, how can we handle this without intruding?

DR. BRAZELTON   I'd just invite them to your house or else say you want to come to them anyway. It's important to them, as it is for you. I'd just ignore the slight and assume that they need and want you. But when you do go, don't wear out your welcome. Make the visit short and offer help. Your presence is both vital and symbolic on important occasions.

QUESTION   What do you think of grandparents as baby-sitters?

DR. BRAZELTON   Wonderful. They are the best. By sitting as often and as regularly as you can, you get to know the children better and they you. At such a time, you fill a needed gap in the nuclear family. You may not find that your children are entirely grateful, for your presence may be more threatening than that of someone whom they pay and about whom the children care less. Children are clever about manipulating their parents with "what Grandma does" or "*she* lets me stay up." So, I'd recognize that it is complicated for your children and remind them that they are in charge. *Listen* to them; don't tell them. They are the parents now.

QUESTION   We live on the East Coast and my family and my husband's live on the West Coast, and it's difficult, even though we see them, to instill that sense of family. I can't call up Gram and say, "Can you come over and watch the kids?" How do we develop that feeling when the distance is so far?

DR. BRAZELTON   Have regular phone times and include the children. Get them to write off and on. And do your best to celebrate major holidays together. No matter what the cost, it's worth it in the long run. Children need to know they have an extended family and people who care about them who are not "just parents." Grandparents and uncles and aunts make a real gift to your children's future.

QUESTION As a child, when I visited my grandparents in another state, I loved going to my father's room. They left the toys just the way they were when he played with them, as if these were the most precious things on earth. My parents have done the same thing, and I love bringing my kids there. My daughter picks up some doll I didn't particularly care for and thinks it's the most valuable thing in the world.

DR. BRAZELTON She values it for its connection with your past. One of the things I most loved as a child was to sit at one of my grandparents' feet and say, "Now, tell me about the olden time." It connects a child with his own history and is more romantic than television.

QUESTION We are immigrants to this country, so most of our family is back home in India. They visit us, but mostly we communicate by pictures.

DR. BRAZELTON Staying in touch is even more critical when you've moved abroad. For your children to grow up in the U.S. as a minority without understanding the strengths and beauty of your own culture would be leaving them without roots. Every minority child deserves as much knowledge of his heritage as the parents can offer, and as much connection as possible with his extended family. Pictures, letters, even recordings which can be sent back and forth are wonderful ways to preserve the ties. I'd also make sure your children are bilingual.

QUESTION   My parents and my in-laws both live in the same town as we do, and our two-year-old is the only in-town grandchild. Every holiday that comes up, I'm like a rubber band. We have to be at my parents' house, and then at my in-laws' house, trying to spend equal time. It's hard.

DR. BRAZELTON   But it's so important to all three of you, as well as to each set of grandparents. Your child may feel bounced about, but she is a lucky girl, and I'd let her know how many people care about her.

The Cutler Family Revisited

Driving into the country to see the Cutlers, I wondered how any parent could deal with commuting an hour each way to work, as I knew Robin had done. Robin had told me how she always arrived home after Wiley's dinner and left before his breakfast, wistful about how much she had missed. During that time, Chris, who had shifted jobs to one close by, shared much of the parenting. Robin had been running her own design consulting firm at the time, and it had been too demanding and rewarding to give up. Now, they had adopted a second baby, and I wondered what the family constellation would be. I had heard that Chris's job had become more demanding during this time. As a senior manager in a large teaching hospital in Worcester, he now was facing the task of merging three smaller local hospitals under the wing of this large institution, a major challenge. I wondered whether he would be willing to cut down now, as he had in Wiley's infancy?

When I arrived at their beautiful modern house in the woods near Worcester, I could see another reason why Robin had been willing to commute. It is serene, spacious, and elegant. A young family couldn't afford such a place if it were nearer a big city. As I drove up to the brightly lit house, five-year-old Wiley was in the doorway waiting for me, although it was past his bedtime. He is the same winning little boy that I remember, except that now he is tall and slender. He still looks much like his father, even though he is adopted. Wiley greeted me like an old and trusted friend, with a big smile: "We've got Sam!" Sam is a two-and-a-half-year-old whom they adopted as a newborn – and right from Worcester, which has one of the highest rates of unwed teenage pregnancy in the country. Most of these young women do not want to keep their babies, but they do want to choose the kind of family into which the baby will go. Although they are not introduced to the adoptive parents, they are told enough about them to make a choice about where the baby will be raised. Giving these young women a choice and getting the baby into a good home right away –

avoiding the usual four-month wait in a foster home – is termed an "ideal adoption." The social workers who work with the teenage mothers become the contact for both the birth mother and the adoptive family.

It is no wonder that the birth mother of Sam chose this family. They are stable and successful; above all, each parent is a caring, nurturing person. As an older brother, Wiley is a testimony to this. Wiley is thoughtful and self-assured. He won me all over again with his warm welcome. His second statement to me was "Here's Bommer just to see you."

If there were any reason for second thoughts about giving a baby to this family, it would quickly be dispelled by an introduction to Wiley's Bommer. She is the ideal grandmother. After I saw her relationship with Wiley, I tried to imitate her with my own grandchild. She offered Wiley a world of dreams, which no small boy could resist. I told the family that I'd been looking forward to my next meeting with Bommer, and Wiley knew this. She'd come up from Cape Cod to be there for my visit. Wiley held her hand as they led me into the two-story living room.

The Cutlers had thoughtfully arranged a place for me to interview them. They had food to welcome me. I felt very close to them all over again. They'd even provided a small mattress nearby for Wiley to collapse on, "so he won't have to miss anything." This way, he could participate as long as he wanted to and could then fall asleep without going away. He felt this was his show, and his parents respected this feeling.

Wiley showed me his schoolbook as well as the drawing he'd made while he waited for me. He conducted our interview, telling me what he'd like to talk about and interrupting me when I wandered off the subject. He watched me carefully to see how I took his comments. He clearly wanted to please me. As we talked about how big he'd gotten, he said seriously, "But I should, I'm older." When we spoke about Sam, he said, "We're glad we got him. We're both adopted, you know." His comments were serious, and I felt they reflected how much communication he'd had with his parents about what I might ask him. He trusted me, I could tell, for he rarely looked back at his parents for reassurance. As we talked, he seemed to get more comfortable. After a few minutes, his rather

The Cutler Family Revisited

still, formal posture gave way to squirming and slumping down in his chair. Then I knew we were friends. He began to tell me more about his school and his friends. When he demonstrated his wonderful sense of humor, his smile was so much like his father's that I gasped. He had the same glint in his eye and the same crinkled upturn of one side of his mouth. Once again I was struck by how secure Wiley was in his masculinity and image of himself, how firmly identified with Chris.

I look for such evidence of identification and of clear attachment to parents when I'm assessing a child I don't know. Does he have a secure-looking stride as he enters the room? Does she imitate either parent with her walk or her gestures? Where does he turn when he's stressed – to his parents, to his blanket or "lovey" or to his thumb? Can the child master a new situation comfortably by herself? Does he have a sense of humor? One of the most telltale signs of stressed children is that they lose their ability to laugh at the world and at themselves. Does she appeal to you? If so, is it because you want to nurture and protect her, or is it because you enjoy and admire her sense of herself? Do other children like him, and does he try to please them? A child who is having a tough time is often avoided by other children because they sense his distress.

Wiley had all the positive attributes, and I could feel his caring and his attachment to everyone around him. At one point he came around the table and drew a chair up close to me to show me pictures of Sam, since "he is already asleep and you'll miss him." My heart was won. I said, "But Wiley, he looks like he might tease people a lot." Wiley looked at me seriously. As we went on talking, he watched me as if to see how far he could trust me. Then he ventured, "Sometimes I wish we'd sent him back." I felt we were really communicating now. I tried to push him a little further, but he'd gone to his limit. He pulled back and changed the subject, pointing to another picture in the album. In the next picture, he tried to show me how funny Sam was. He'd demonstrated as much of his inner struggle as he could. It isn't Wiley's style to complain or to show his feelings too easily. He is a boy who thinks and feels deeply. He contains any negative feelings he might have and handles them himself. Then he can present a cheery exterior, which wins a response from everyone around him. Is it costly for him? He is certainly easy on the surface; he's lovable and wins your heart. I could wish for a little less compliance. I hope he can learn to turn some of his feelings outward, so they won't cost him too much.

Chris and Robin are aware of Wiley's reserve. Sam is very different and has made them see that not all children are like Wiley. He is forceful and openly demanding. He pushes Wiley constantly, as the older boy tries to contain his feelings about his easily aggressive, provocative little brother. Whereas Wiley tries to please everyone, Sam bombs his way through everything to get what he wants. He's so physical that when he does think or talk about something, it comes as a surprise. Robin commented on the difference. "Thank God he's bright. You might not know it when he's being so active and aggressive. When he lets you see it, he's got a very quick, exciting little mind." Even as she talked, I sensed that this child was easy for her to understand and to relate to.

We talked about the differences between the two boys. Wiley, like his father, keeps his feelings to himself. Sam's behavior fits the slang expression, "letting it all hang out." This constellation is common — an older child burying feelings and appearing eager to please on the surface, and a second child who is more open, direct, aggressive. I pointed out to Robin and Chris that Sam might always be easy to understand and would demand what he needed from everyone around him. Adjusting to stress would be less costly for him than for Wiley. Wiley would be likely to try to handle it all by himself. In the long run, he'd be harder for them to understand and to help when he was in trouble. To balance this, Wiley had a wonderful, secure relationship with both parents and obviously had a very sure self-image. In addition, Wiley's close identification with his father meant that Chris had a lot of empathy for how he might be feeling. They could work things out together, for they were on the same wavelength. "But I want to be in on this, too," said Robin. I could assure her that she would be. Wiley

The Cutler Family Revisited

looks at her with devotion. With her more ebullient temperament, she can teach him to open up and to get things out on the surface. She can help him learn to let up on himself.

"Actually," said Robin, "Sam is teaching him to be bad. Wiley tells proud stories about Sam's being bad. That's a first step, isn't it? And he's begun to let it out at home. He is just beginning to beat up on Sam, to talk back to me, even to scream and to kick when he's angry. It's almost as if he's imitating Sam. But he always looks to be sure he hasn't gone too far. That's still pretty self-conscious, isn't it?"

I agreed with her that when Wiley stopped worrying so much about what everyone else wanted of him, he'd be better off, and that Sam was a wonderful, balancing influence. Sam is teaching him to fight back, to be bad when he needs to. It will be important that no one land too hard on Wiley when he shows his feelings openly. He may well have to try out some pretty aggressive things on Sam and with his parents. He may have to swing wide to reach the middle. Not only will his outbursts be likely to surprise everyone around him, for they will be so out of character, but they may even shock his parents at their apparent ferocity. But in the long run, he will benefit if they can allow him to test the limits and to let up on himself. They mustn't pull away into permissiveness completely, however. Discipline and limits will reassure him until he learns comfortable ones for himself. At the point where he's getting out of hand, he'll need them to say something along these lines: "Wiley, we want you to show us how you feel, and to be tough and strong, but this is as far as you can go. This is enough. When you can't stop yourself, we can and will." This assurance, given in a firm but understanding way, can be comforting to a child like Wiley. Otherwise, his "new" aggressive feelings could frighten him.

Wiley's style of being aware of others and ready to please will serve him well for the future. These qualities are common ones in successful people. So I would certainly not want him to lose them. But if he can balance them with a sense of how and when to let off steam, they will have less internal costs for him in the future. Wiley is a wonderful little boy. Robin and Chris showed their justifiable pride as they spoke to me about him.

The Cutler Family

"Wiley was such a normal little baby," said Robin. "After all the horror we'd been through in trying to have one of our own, he seemed unbelievable. From the first, he seemed to sense that we needed to understand him, and he'd show us. He was our magical child, and we both felt blessed." As Robin talked, both of them leaned forward as if to impress me with their earnestness and their gratitude to Wiley. Shortly before, he had gone over to his mattress to lie down. He had reached for his beloved teddy bear, pulled up his blanket to curl up in a ball, and gone quietly to sleep. As they talked of him in almost religious voices, they looked over at him. Indeed, the beautiful little boy sleeping there did have something miraculous about him.

There is a set of parental emotions that those of us who work with families call the "Christ child syndrome." Many parents feel it about one child or another, usually the first child. Often it is enhanced, as in Robin and Chris's case, by difficulty in conceiving and producing the first child, or by experiences in the parents' own past which led them not to expect a normal, healthy baby. Mothers who are displaced from their own families cling to a first child as if he or she were their salvation. Parents who have experienced an impaired brother or sister are unconsciously prepared for a less-than-perfect offspring. When the new baby turns out normal and healthy, they idealize him or her. Such children are showered with necessary and welcome attention, but this can be coupled with an expectation that they be perfect in their behavior. Very early, these children sense how they must please their parents, and they learn to be good on the surface. The cost of such a pattern is not always apparent, and it may not even be pronounced enough to worry about. The question to ask is: Does this child expect too much of himself? Is she too much of a perfectionist? Can he allow himself to fail without feeling overwhelmed?

Robin then went on to say that Sam's arrival had brought them down to earth. "This is very different. None of the romance and magic I felt with Wiley, just hard work and wondering when I'll ever have enough time again in my life. I have no more illusions about wanting a third, not even 'one of my own.' There aren't any choices with Sam. I can't see the forest for the trees with him. He's so demanding and so physical. I spank. I *never* thought I would. I scold. I'd have *never* done that to Wiley. I can say, 'You little devil,' and mean it. Is that more like natural parents? I think it is. With Wiley, we just blended. We both wanted him to be 'ours.' This seems to be unnecessary with Sam. Neither of us wants to admit he's like us. And yet he is. I feel very much simpatico with him. I feel just like him. It's so amazing that you can love two children so differently and so passionately!"

"By now we are not aware of the distinction between natural and adoptive parents," said Chris. "We are submerged in parenting. Sam makes us feel like we've made it. There's nothing magical about him. We'd wanted a girl, but when the social worker called me in the midst of a big conference, I didn't have a moment's hesitation. They brought him to us in a big blue van. Sometimes Wiley says, 'Get that van to take him away!'"

At this point Robin said, "I've stayed home with him. I don't want to miss as much as I did with Wiley. I need to be home for both children. That commute was too horrible. I can get part-time consulting out here, and then I won't miss so much with my boys."

I've heard this story many times before. Many parents find that they can go back to full-time work after the first child, but not after the second. Either they feel that they want to savor the experiences with the second that they've missed with the first, or they find that two are considerably more demanding than one. Robin's reappraisal and decision to stay home is common.

"I've even thought of changing jobs," said Robin, "from an interior designer to a teacher. I am thinking of going to art school in order to work with children. I'd like to play around, to finger-paint, to make messy sculptures. Sam has given me permission to be less than perfect. Before Sam, I felt afraid to read about child rearing. I didn't dare overanalyze for fear of failing. I wanted to do so right by Wiley. Adoptive parents feel the need to be perfect. I was even afraid his parents would think I'd failed him. I don't feel that with Sam. He gives me room for error. He's given me a second chance. I can be *me* now."

As both parents described how deeply involved they felt, I could sense how closely identified each was with one of the boys. Robin was describing how easily her personality fits with Sam's. I already knew that Chris feels the same way about Wiley. Each boy is fortunate in having two parents. Their relationships with each are not worse or better, but different. All parents feel differently about different children. It is a fallacy to think that one must have the same or even an equal relationship with each child. Relationships that matter are built on reactions which are too deep-seated to control in such an intellectual way. What Robin and Chris can do is to recognize this, and to value it. Then they can share the raising of each boy in ways that profit from these different relationships. For example, Robin is likely to be direct and unemotional about setting limits for Sam. Afterward, she'll understand how he feels, and can gather him up to comfort him. After the episode is over, I hope she'll use her closeness to let him see why discipline and limits are important. He's liable to learn easily and quickly from her direct approach with him. Wiley may well learn limits more easily from Chris, who can give him insight into how he learned his own limits as a child.

At this point, Bommer joined in. She'd been elsewhere, respectful of their time with me. However, she knew I wanted to hear her side of it all, too.

"How did you get your name?" I asked. "Was it from older grandchildren?"

"No, it was from Wiley," she replied. "I do have two sons, and each has children. One granddaughter and two grandsons, in addition to Wiley and Sam. I adore all of them – all differently. But Wiley gets to me in a special way, I guess. I felt part of his miracle. I wanted him so much for Chris and Robin. When he arrived, I was so delighted. And he has never let me down.

"I got my name when he was one and a half. We were watching airplanes go over. I said, 'Look at that old bomber!' Later that evening, he remembered the words and attached them to me. It stuck! No one else has an old Bommer for a grandmother. I love it."

She told me how she was left a widow when her children were very young. She had to make a living, so she went back to school herself and then taught dyslexic children at a private school. One son was dyslexic, which motivated her to choose this kind of teaching. As a single parent, she raised all three children. "It wasn't easy. But it was exciting. And in a way, they probably raised

The Cutler Family Revisited

themselves. Don't let anyone tell you there aren't advantages. These kids grew so close to each other because they had to. They all know how to cook, to clean, to take care of others. They had to. We were a stressed, working family all right, but they all learned from it." In her words, I felt the strength and passion which she'd handed on to her children.

As she talked of her relationship with Wiley, I could also feel that it was free of the stress she experienced while shouldering the whole responsibility for her own children. One of the particular delights of being a grandparent is that you can free up the pleasure of parenting from the responsibility. Grandparents can leave the teaching, the drill, to someone else. They are free to enjoy the world anew with a grandchild and to sit back and admire the child's growth.

"Wiley and I get along very well," said Bommer. "We always have. We have tea parties, we spend hours talking and imagining. Everything we do is imaginary. When we see-saw, we dream we are on a ship and are off to South Sea Islands. We go to dance with the natives. He dances and I dance. We laugh at each other's dancing and imagine how much better the natives are at dancing. We sing about almost everything. I'd never sing with anyone else. We also make up words, sometimes ones no one else can understand. We live in a world of our own."

As this extraordinary grandmother talked, her eyes danced, and how much they communicated! They took me off into that imaginary world. I could see that she offered Wiley a dimension of life which parents aren't likely to offer. I would never have dared be this free and imaginative with my own children. I would have been afraid of taking them away from the "real" world with which they would have to deal. Parents worry when their children are too involved in a dream world. But here was Bommer, daring to lead this boy into an exotic land of music and dancing and imaginary languages. How tawdry and flat a television show would be in comparison. Wiley's view of the world and its possibilities was made wider and more exciting, thanks to this lovely grandmother. And so was hers:

"You can see how he's enriched my life," said Bommer. "I came up to stay with him while Chris and Robin went to a New

Year's Eve party. I never put him to bed because I wanted his company. We began to make resolutions. He was only two, but we thought up about ten resolutions each. Finally he said, 'Isn't this a party?' I answered, 'Yes.' He said, 'Then, I'm thirsty.' I got him some ginger ale. He smacked his lips, settled back in his chair, and said, 'Now I'm ready to talk some more!' I laughed and laughed. We made some Christmas 'worms.' When I asked him what kind of cookies he wanted to make, he said, 'Just worms.' He was so proud of them that he went off to get his beloved blanket. He showed his blanket the cookies: 'You may look, but don't touch them.' He is so serious and so bright. I couldn't ever feel as special about another child, I fear. I worry about that, but not much. Wiley is my magical child!"

Wiley is indeed fortunate. Bommer epitomizes that fourth dimension a grandparent brings to a child — a world of fantasy and reality mixed, an opportunity to try out things without any retaliation or any agenda for learning. Her task and Wiley's is to share the magic of every day — old and young together.

The Cooper Family

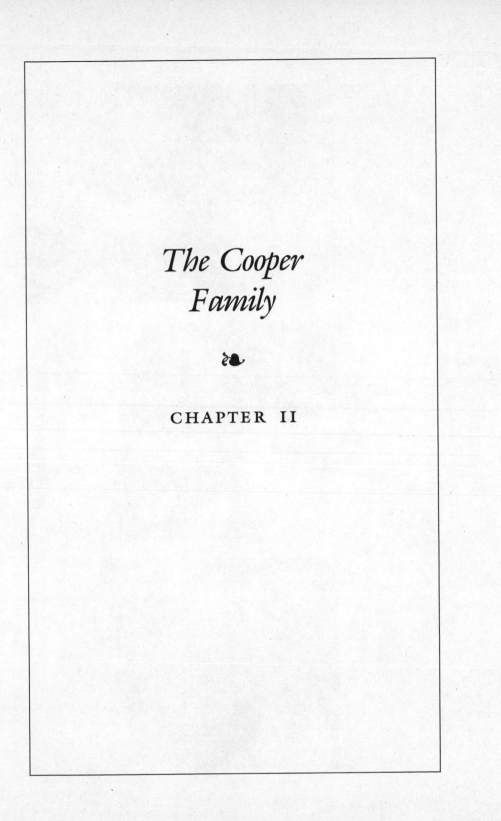

CHAPTER II

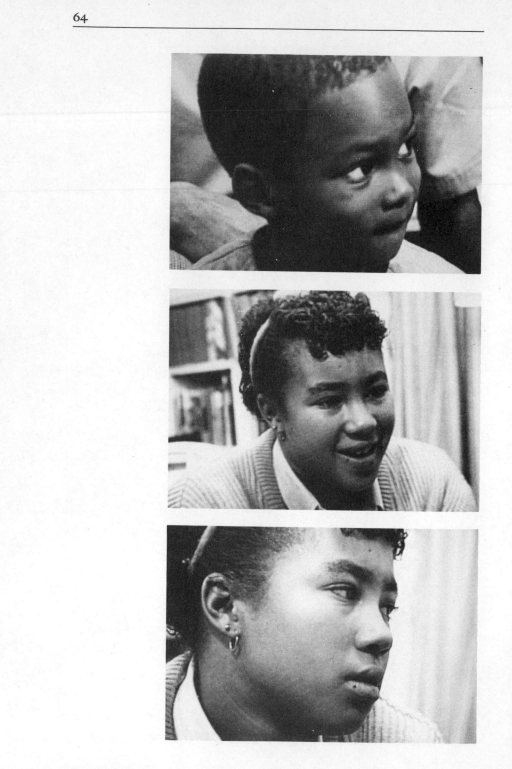

The Cooper Family

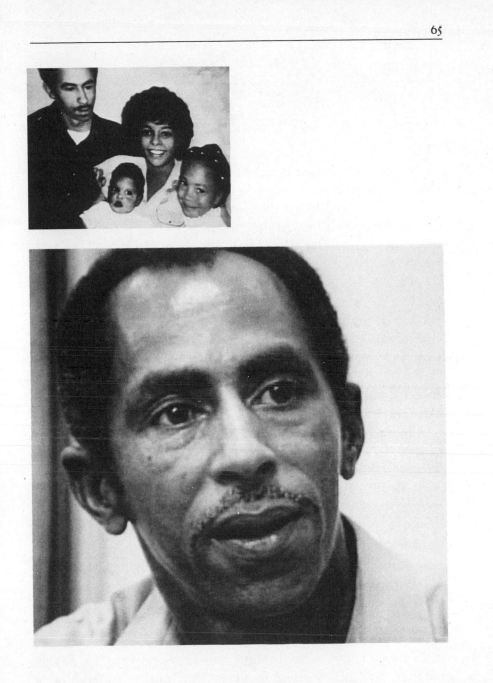

The Cooper Family

Family History

❧

Charles Cooper is a single parent. His wife died two years before we first met, when their daughter Yolanda was ten and their second child, Charles, Jr., was two. She died of cancer after a long illness in which she "tried to hang on in order to raise her children." Charles worshiped her. In the middle of his living room wall is a touching photograph of a lovely young black woman with an earnest expression.

Charles is a policeman in Framingham, an affluent suburb of Boston. He is one of the few black men on the town payroll. He is not a large man, but is trim and muscular, obviously in perfect condition. One whole wall of his apartment is filled with trophies – he's a champion bowler. Soon after meeting him, I was impressed by the strength of his personality, his seriousness and sincerity. He appeared sure of himself, determined to succeed in a white, often unwelcoming world. There was no doubt about his dedication to his children. As he talked to me, his eyes were constantly taking in Charles, Jr.'s, and Yolanda's reactions. He touched young Charles tenderly as the four-year-old climbed onto his lap. He leaned toward Yolanda, twelve at that time, as he talked about her. As we spoke about his concerns, about how to carry out his wife's dreams for their children, I could see that the memory of his wife has become a model for them all, encouraging them to aspire high.

Charles has taken on a dual role: both mothering and fathering. When I visited, I could see that he combines both tenderness and a firm manner, a mixture of nurturance and authority. In no way is he anything but a strong, masculine figure, but this is tempered with warmth and closeness. He is *the parent*, and Charles and Yolanda know it. Both children obviously respect him. As they talked to me, they watched him from time to time to see how he was reacting.

Charles's mother lives with the family. She is quite elderly and not able to help very much in the care either of the house or of the children. Charles is trying to get her into a nursing home, but is finding it difficult because she is black. He talked of this without rancor, but I sensed his determination to overcome the color barrier.

Charles Cooper seems to me a man of extraordinary physical and moral stamina. He is coping with a situation that would overwhelm many parents. Charles works eight hours each night, patrolling. His shift is from 11:45 P.M. to 8:10 A.M., but he manages to get home briefly early in the morning to get the children up and off to school. After he gets off at 8:10, he does the shopping, cleans the house, does the necessary laundry, and tends to his mother's needs. If there's any time left before Charles, Jr., comes home in the early afternoon, he can take a nap. When Yolanda comes home, she takes over while he sleeps. She makes dinner and helps with the cleaning up. In the evening, he makes time for them both and helps with their homework.

Loss of a Parent

୬

HOME VISIT

When I first met the Cooper family, I visited them at home to learn first-hand about their family situation. After hearing from Charles about his incredible schedule, I asked him how he got enough sleep.

CHARLES   I don't, but have learned to survive on what I get. Sleeping in the daytime can easily be interrupted by what is going on with the children.

DR. BRAZELTON   Can your mother help out with any of the day-to-day housework?

CHARLES   She did for a while after my wife died. She tided us over the worst times. But now she's really not equal to it – mentally or physically. I feel like we wore her out.

DR. BRAZELTON   But you're wearing yourself out.

CHARLES   I'm going to get these kids through the most difficult age. My wife left me with a challenge – to give them a real start in life. She was the most wonderful woman, and she really struggled to stay alive. She gave these kids all she could before she died. Now it's up to me.

DR. BRAZELTON   Will you get married again?

CHARLES   I haven't got time to think about it. I can't replace her, I know that. I'm going full blast.

The Cooper Family

I do have my bowling, and I love to fish. I hope someday to have a boat for the family so we can all fish together. They go with me everywhere on the weekends. Charles follows me around pretty close. He never lets me out of his sight when I'm around. He won't even go to sleep unless I'm there and holding on to him.

As his father talked, Charles, Jr., snuggled in even closer. During my visit, he had not strayed far from his father. Charles, Sr., cradled him in his arms. He is a clear-eyed, thoughtful little boy, obviously not in serious trouble, but I did wonder about his rather immature behavior.

DR. BRAZELTON   Does he play with other kids?

CHARLES   Some. But he's pretty clinging. Should I worry?

DR. BRAZELTON   Well, it does seem like it may be a result of losing his mother. Has he ever asked you much about her?

CHARLES   He was only two when she died. But she devoted all her time to him. Is he missing her? We sure do.

DR. BRAZELTON   I think you may need to discuss it with him from time to time. This is an age when fears – of loss, of losing you, and yearning for a mother figure – do surface.

Loss of a Parent

THE ISSUES

Before a family can recover fully from the loss of one parent, each person must recognize what the loss means. In particular, the widowed spouse must address his or her own grief. Before he can help Yolanda and Charles, Jr., with their side, Charles, Sr., must be allowed to grieve and to heal his own wounds. He has managed to protect himself so far by submerging himself in work: his eight-hour shift, followed by every chore in his household. He's had to parent his own infirm mother as well as a preteenager and a four-year-old. The constant demands of two full-time jobs leave him no time to attend to his own feelings. Many bereaved spouses take shelter in work. During the acute grieving period, they set themselves endless demands. Eventually it is necessary to slow down, to limit the working hours, even to share some of the work, and to allow themselves to grieve. One of the dangers of not facing grief is that parents will hold on to the children too tightly for their own good. They are bound to be afraid of losing their children as well. When grief is faced and allowed to heal, then bereaved parents find it easier to loosen their grasp on the children.

The next step is to help each child understand and face his or her particular loss. This is different for every child. A very young child such as Charles, Jr., will not be able to talk about his fears and sadness. But there are certain universal feelings for a young child in this situation, and the surviving parent can watch and listen for them:

1. A feeling of being different, of having an incomplete family, especially when with children who do have intact families
2. Fear of losing the surviving parent, seen in anxiety about new situations or separations
3. A delusion of having caused the death, resulting in feelings of guilt
4. Hunger for an adult the same sex as the lost parent
5. Anger at the surviving parent for not providing a mother or father

6. Regression to a more infantile stage of development when new stresses must be faced

7. Possessiveness toward the surviving parent and jealousy of his or her relationships

Many of these feelings and the resulting behavior can be seen in Charles, Jr., and will gradually emerge in most children who lose a parent in the early years of life.

Charles, Jr., can hardly remember his lost mother. As he gets older, he will need a female around to help him sort out his own male identity. Yolanda can serve that purpose for him if she is present and cares for him. But a girl her age will need to become more independent and to rebel herself. At four years old, Charles, Jr., has also lost the secure base which allows aggression to surface. If his mother's death leaves him overshadowed with fears — fear of another loss (his father, grandmother, or Yolanda), or fear of being bad (imagining that by misbehaving he may have caused his mother's death) — his development could be endangered.

Part of Charles, Jr.'s, clinging may be reinforced by his father's own loneliness. The boy senses this and finds his demands for closeness are readily answered. Feeling his father's longings and not daring to act up for fear of losing another parent, Charles, Jr., may not develop the independence and autonomy that is natural at this age. Eventually he must feel secure enough to separate, and his father must recover enough from his own loss to allow this.

If the parent who has died is never discussed, children are deprived of the opportunity to share grief. This heightens their feelings of isolation and their fear of further loss. Children young Charles's age can't conceive of death as a reality. To them, death sounds like sleep. Four-year-olds believe that you can wake up from it, or come alive if people wish hard enough. After all, television cartoons confirm this. Heroes get up and walk away. Small children carry this fantasy one step farther. If they are good enough, maybe they might be able to bring the lost parent back. If they are the least bit bad, they will keep her away and assure the family of continuing grief. Such fantasies give children three choices: to be very good and try to prove the thesis; to be very bad and test the system; or to withdraw into being so immature that good and bad are not an issue. Charles seemed to be regressed and clinging, as if he were trying to stay a baby and to prove how innocent his behavior was.

When a child has a chance to ask questions, "What is death? Where is Mommy? Did I make it happen? Does she see me from up there? Does she still love me?" the need for denial and aggression gradually fades. Most children ask some of these questions, but they need to be repeated over and over. The parent of a child as young as Charles will have to push him to be on his own a bit more, to give him permission to express his fears. Such a child may need to try out a bit of aggression, and to find out that he won't break any magical bubble if he is testy and bad at times. A peer group at school also helps. For a child whose mother has died, an understanding, caring female teacher with whom he can relate, whom he can test and then trust, would be a major asset.

For a girl Yolanda's age, the issues are different. She has been asked to take over part of her mother's role. As a female, and older, she was naturally drawn into this responsibility, and also into being a mother figure for her brother. If she doesn't help in both of these areas, she will feel guilty. The need is too obvious. However, as a normal preadolescent, she will have to rebel off and on. She will have to groan, to complain, to leave her work unfinished, to anger her father. If she doesn't, there will be a serious cost to her. Her own identity as separate from her family is formed by this kind of rebellion. If she is able to suppress all of her rebellion, she might have to pay for it by acting out later. She, too, has anxieties about why her mother died, about death itself, about how much she contributed to her mother's illness. She needs a chance to talk about them.

If the bereaved parent can make time to hear her concerns, a girl Yolanda's age will feel she can communicate about the other issues of adolescence which are surely coming. If the parent can tolerate only good behavior, she will have to work out her rebellion elsewhere or in less acceptable ways. She may begin to stay out too late, to turn to less desirable friends, or even to run away, as proof that she has an independent existence. If she has unresolved grief about losing her mother, she is more likely to test her father, to express her anger at "Why me?" A widowed parent must be prepared for this. The sooner he can begin to share his own grief with her and let her share her grief openly, the freer he will be to accept her normal adolescent rebellion.

The following are suggestions for parents who must help a child face the death or loss of the other parent:

- Children need to be reassured over and over that they are loved, and were loved by the absent parent.
- Children need to hear repeatedly that they hadn't any responsibility for the death of the parent. They need to know that they can be "bad" without losing the surviving parent.
- At the same time, children do need firm limits. Limits are reassuring.
- Grief should be addressed and shared openly.
- Teachers and close friends should be advised, so that they can help the child adjust.
- Other changes in plans, schedules, and surroundings should be minimized.
- Older children can take much responsibility but must be reassured that they needn't try to replace the dead spouse.
- The occasion of death is an important time to pass on a family's basic belief systems – about religion, about death, about the afterlife. There will be unanswerable questions, of course, but a parent can explain his or her beliefs and how they have helped in facing the loss.
- Parents should never be afraid to express their own grief in front of children. This helps establish the reality of death. Even a father needs to cry and to share his feelings. Children may feel obligated to offer comfort. Parents should accept this comfort, but assure the children that they can handle their sorrow.
- Children should be allowed to grieve at their own pace. They will mourn for years, but off and on. An adult will mourn more intensely but heal over time. As soon as a parent feels able, he or she can help by offering children safe ways and special times to share their grief. Visiting a grave, sitting down to look over letters and photos – these are among the possible

Loss of a Parent

ways to remember the dead. If children aren't ready, or if they don't want to share, that should be respected, too. Timing has to be individual.

- If the symptoms of clinging and fears continue, or the adolescent rebellion is too overwhelming, parents should consider counseling – not as a sign of failure, but as a source of strength in facing a crisis which is more than most families will ever have to face.

COMMON QUESTIONS

QUESTION   If an adult is in a lot of pain, how can she help her child?

DR. BRAZELTON   I'm not sure you can at that time, except by being close and by being reliably present. If you are absent, it scares the child. When you recover somewhat, you can then turn your attention to the child's issues. Fortunately, children not only have a strong sense of denial which will tide them over, but they also are able to postpone their reaction to a loss until adults around them can stand it. But *then* they need your help.

QUESTION   I didn't take my daughter to her mother's funeral, but now I do take her to the grave. Is this right?

DR. BRAZELTON   Funerals are for closure and are for adults. They help us accept death and help bring to a close the reality of life. If children asked to go, I would take them, but someone should be with them to attend to their questions and their anxieties. Taking your daughter with you when you go to pay homage to your wife's grave seems to me a good thing for both of you. It is a real opportunity to share your grief and your beliefs, and to discuss the inevitability of death as a part of life. The more you can share with her, the better. Be sure to listen to her side of it.

QUESTION   My son lost his father when he was two. How can I reassure him that I won't die, as well?

DR. BRAZELTON   You must raise the issue by saying, "I know you worry about that. You're bound to, but I'm *not* going to die. I'm going to stay right here with you." He needs to hear it over and over.

QUESTION   My wife was sick for a long time. I tried to shelter my daughter. Was this wrong?

DR. BRAZELTON   I don't think you can shelter a child from reality. You can still go back over it all with her and tell her all you remember. Go slowly and answer all her questions. Listen to her fears and face them with her. For her to face them all alone is lonely and scary. Facing them with you isn't.

QUESTION   My son, who is four, wants me to answer "Where's Mommy?" with a specific place. What can I say?

DR. BRAZELTON   A child three to six is very concrete in his thinking. Just as primitive peoples designate heaven and hell as places on a map, children want a specific answer. Of course, you can't give her one, and I'd say so honestly. But you can dream together about where she might be.

Loss of a Parent

Listen to what he imagines and, at the same time, explain any belief systems you may have. He will value your honesty and your attention more than any one answer.

QUESTION   My son lost his older brother. He asked *why* he had to die. What can anyone say to that?

DR. BRAZELTON   Behind the philosophical question are specific ones you can answer. Explain your older son's illness in terms he can understand. Perhaps he is asking whether it was partly his fault, or he may also wonder whether he will die, too. You *can* answer those questions. After explaining what you do know, open it up for him to ask you about what still bothers him. What's behind his questions may be more important than what you hear on the surface.

QUESTION   My daughter seems to be waiting for her sister to come back – or for us to replace her.

DR. BRAZELTON   This is an example of concrete thinking. You can say, "We all wish she'd come back. She won't, but we can keep her alive in our minds. Maybe that way, she'll know we are thinking about her, and we'll feel her close by." You can assure her that a replacement wouldn't be the same and that you want to wait until you're recovered somewhat before you even think about another baby. You want that baby to be special on her own, and not just a replacement for her sister.

QUESTION   Since my husband died, my son seems to want to be a baby again. Is that natural?

The Cooper Family

DR. BRAZELTON   Yes. A regression is a very normal and very healthy way for a child to cope. This is also a plea to you to help him understand his feelings about losing his father.

QUESTION   My child was two when her mother died. How do I know how much she remembers and understands?

DR. BRAZELTON   I'm not sure you can ever really know. All you can do is listen to her concerns and watch what she shows you in her behavior. When you tell her about her mother, listen for her side.

QUESTION   My son was four when his dad died. He recently said he doesn't remember his father anymore.

DR. BRAZELTON   He may be repressing memories that are painful. They may return later when he can handle them. He may be trying to get you to tell him more about his father. At any rate, I'd make a point of talking about his father, asking him to reminisce with you about what he was like and how your son resembles him. He may need to know more about his father as he gets older in order to identify with him and develop his own masculine identity as separate from yours.

QUESTION   Are nightmares connected with loss? How should a parent deal with them?

DR. BRAZELTON   Nightmares and fears often arise long after a death, at a time when a child is beginning to be ready to deal with the loss. They signal to you as a parent to listen to the child's anxieties. Let her know you understand. Take her fears

Loss of a Parent

and nightmares seriously enough to go in and comfort her. Give her a night light or favorite soft toy to take to bed, if they help. During the day, talk about her fears and the grief you both feel. Then help her see that they are behind the nightmares. Give her as much insight as you think she can use. Helping a child understand her own reactions not only reassures her, it also teaches her to use insight as a way of handling stress.

QUESTION

My grandmother, who was an invalid and rather dotty, just died. I feel it is a mercy, but should I say this to the children?

DR. BRAZELTON

Losing a grandparent or great-grandparent isn't easy, even when she's infirm and a burden to the family. Being honest about your own feelings always helps. You can explain that old people come to a place in life where death is a relief and a release. It's harder on us than on them. You probably miss the person she once was. Encourage everyone to remember all they can about her. Let guilty feelings emerge. Allow yourself to feel sorrow about what you didn't do for your grandmother and wish you'd done. Death is difficult to understand, but it is a part of living. If it can be faced honestly and together, as a family, it can become a source of strength.

Fathering Alone

৯▲

OFFICE VISIT

The Cooper family came into my office, apparently for a checkup for Charles, Jr. At first he was too frightened to let me examine him. I changed the focus to his father and how they were coping. I suggested that we use the visit to get acquainted more and save the examination and shots until after Charles got to know and trust me. In that way, he could let me become his friend and his doctor. A child of four is bound to see a physical exam as an invasion. After a personal tragedy and loss, it is even more threatening.

DR. BRAZELTON Hi, Coopers. Welcome. Hello, Charles. You're big now, aren't you? How old are you?

CHARLES, JR. Four.

DR. BRAZELTON You brought your big sister with you. That's *good*.

CHARLES, JR. Don't touch me.

DR. BRAZELTON Charles, for a checkup, I'll have to touch you *some*. But you don't want me to touch you now. Would you rather come another time when we know each other better? I want to be your friend as well as your doctor. *Turning to Charles, Sr.* Are you still on the night shift?

CHARLES Yes, it has its good points as far as the kids are concerned, because I'm home during the daytime. I think I'm closer to my son than other fathers would be. When my wife died, he was pretty close to her. And he hasn't forgotten her. From the time she had her operation and they discovered that she had cancer, everything she did mostly centered around Charles, Jr. I mean, she taught him a lot. When my wife was living, she was a heck of a woman. I don't know how to explain it. She was the best. *Charles pauses.* Keeping the family together without a mother is one of the hardest things I've ever done. I have to be mother, father, sister, brother, friend, and housekeeper and everything else.

DR. BRAZELTON   Can Yolanda help you? *Yolanda nods.*

CHARLES   Yolanda sometimes becomes like a mother to Charles. She gets him dressed; sometimes she gives him baths at night before he goes to bed.

DR. BRAZELTON   That's great. How is Charles doing now?

CHARLES   He seems to hold on to me, you know. Wherever I go, he wants to go. Single fathers have a tough time. There are certain things that just don't come together as if I were a mother. My family to me is the most important thing in my life. Everything I do, they do with me. If I don't take them with me, then it's not done. Between working at night and the kids – doing things around the house – it's rough.

DR. BRAZELTON   *To Charles, Jr.* How's your daddy doing?

CHARLES, JR.   Fine.

DR. BRAZELTON   Is he like a mommy to you?

CHARLES, JR.   Hmmm hmmmm.

The Cooper Family

DR. BRAZELTON   He has to be, doesn't he?

CHARLES   I don't know what I'm going to do next. I go through the daily routine, but, you know, if I don't do everything around my house, nothing gets done. Nothing *moves* unless *I* move.

DR. BRAZELTON   But you seem to find time for the kids.

CHARLES   When Charles comes home at noon, I can give him a little time. And when Yolanda gets home, if she starts her homework right away, I help her with her homework.

DR. BRAZELTON   *To Yolanda*. And you help your father?

YOLANDA   Well, I help sometimes.

DR. BRAZELTON   Sometimes?

YOLANDA   Sometimes, yeah, because I'm trying to get my schoolwork done and trying to watch over Charles, too. While my father sleeps, Charles is running around outside, and all these things'll be happening, you know, and I'm trying to make sure he's around the house.

DR. BRAZELTON   Good for you, Yolanda. It's not easy at your age, is it? Hey, Charles. Tell me something about you.

CHARLES, JR.   I don't help around the house.

DR. BRAZELTON   What do you do?

CHARLES, JR.   I don't mess the house up.

Fathering Alone

DR. BRAZELTON You help your daddy that way, then, huh? Do you ever help him clean?

CHARLES, JR. Mmmmm mmmmm.

DR. BRAZELTON And cooking?

CHARLES, JR. Unh unh! No!

DR. BRAZELTON Why?

CHARLES, JR. 'Cause I might burn the food up. *Yolanda is laughing in the background.*

Charles and Yolanda both did what they could, but it was still pretty rough on their father.

CHARLES I take it one day at a time. I go through that day, and tomorrow I do tomorrow. That seems to be the ticket right now.

DR. BRAZELTON Charles, what if you found somebody else to take care of the kids? A lot of men would do that.

CHARLES Actually, I feel that they're my kids, so I have to raise them.

DR. BRAZELTON You feel very strongly about keeping these kids together and keeping the family solid, don't you?

CHARLES Well, when my wife was alive, she used to do mostly everything. I didn't have to do too much. And when she got sick and time grew short, one day we were at the hospital and she said to me, "What are you going to do when I die? I don't think you're going to be able to

The Cooper Family

make it." I said to her and to myself, "I'll make it. We'll make it." This is something that I've got to do for myself. It's something that will make me feel better, because she didn't believe I could do it.

DR. BRAZELTON So you feel as though she's watching over you and you're trying to prove it to her?

CHARLES That's a . . . possibility. I think so. But I didn't have any idea that it was going to be this hard. *She* knew – she knew very well.

DR. BRAZELTON It sounds like you're trying to give these kids what their mother would have given them, and you're playing mother and father at the same time.

CHARLES Sometimes I feel that I'm bumping my head up against a wall. But I believe that my reward is going to come when my kids grow up.

DR. BRAZELTON There will be rewards for them, too. How about you, Yolanda?

YOLANDA My father's teaching me things – how to do things – and if he wasn't here to show me, I probably wouldn't know how to do anything.

DR. BRAZELTON You'd really feel deserted, wouldn't you?

YOLANDA Yeah. *Pointing to Charles, Jr.* He is the only thing I've got now, besides my father.

DR. BRAZELTON That's pretty precious, isn't it? *To Charles.* You know, I think you're really doing it, Charles. You've been able to take the place of both mother and father. The most important thing

Fathering Alone

I see is the example you've given these kids of being responsible for the family. Each of them is playing a role in keeping your family together. Somewhere you must feel awfully good. You've found a good way to handle your terrible loss.

I turned again to Yolanda. I wanted to know how she was dealing with all of this. Almost thirteen, she was beginning to develop physically. She was confronted with puberty and had no mother to turn to. She would need women friends. Could I help as well by letting her know I understood and wanted to be available?

I mentioned to Yolanda that a pediatrician is more than a baby doctor. I'm interested in being a doctor to the whole family.

YOLANDA   I want to be a doctor, too, maybe.

DR. BRAZELTON Do you? That's wonderful! What made you decide?

YOLANDA   My mother, actually. After she died, I was thinking maybe I could help find a cure for cancer.

DR. BRAZELTON That's why most people are doctors, you know. They want to cure the diseases people they loved went through, to keep other people from having to go through them. That's the best reason for being a doctor that I know of. *But there was another reason.* Dad would be proud of that, too, wouldn't he?

CHARLES   I certainly would! *Yolanda seemed to want to talk more.*

The Cooper Family

YOLANDA   I've got to wake up around seven o'clock in the morning to go to school. I'm tired from helping around the house.

DR. BRAZELTON   Do you get angry?

YOLANDA   Yes, sometimes. If I get mad, I'm not able to finish my homework or study for a test, and if I take the test, I'll get a low mark, you know, and that makes me mad. I'm trying to get on the honor roll this year.

DR. BRAZELTON   The honor roll would show your father you're doing your best, wouldn't it? It's really important to you, isn't it? Charles, you've set some very high standards.

CHARLES   They might not get away with a lot of things, but sometimes they do, for instance, Charles, Jr. I spoil him. I spoil him just like I used to spoil Yolanda. I used to spoil them both.

DR. BRAZELTON   You don't feel like you spoil her now?

CHARLES   No! The days of spoiling are over. It's time to get ready for life.

DR. BRAZELTON   Yolanda, you seem to have a feeling of your mother being there – maybe you're doing a lot of these things for her.

YOLANDA   It makes me feel good when people say I look a little bit like her. My brother favors her a little bit more.

DR. BRAZELTON   But you want to be like her? *Yolanda nods yes vigorously.* Do you feel like you have to play mother to Charles?

Fathering Alone

YOLANDA He calls me Mom.

DR. BRAZELTON Does he?

YOLANDA That makes me feel good.

DR. BRAZELTON You're being two different people. You're a sister, but you're also having to play mommy a lot. You're doing fine. For a girl your age to have to play those two roles is a lot to ask.

YOLANDA If I get married and take care of my own, I'll know what to do. I'll be prepared for it.

DR. BRAZELTON You will have been through it once before. You know, I've noticed one thing: your father has his hands full now with your brother. He doesn't have a lot of time for you.

YOLANDA I know he has to pay attention to my brother more because he's smaller.

DR. BRAZELTON Do you feel left out a little bit?

YOLANDA Maybe sometimes. I won't lie.

DR. BRAZELTON You know, to be able to take it like this means you are very grown up. You're an unusual girl. I think your father thinks so, too.

YOLANDA I hope so! He'd better!

The Cooper Family

THE ISSUES

A single parent – mother or father – has a difficult job under any set of circumstances. Parents who are alone feel that they must be everything to each child. They try to be superparents – an impossible dream. Each deviation on the child's part is likely to be taken as a sign of personal failure. Successes are likely to be ignored, while failures stand out. The single parents in my practice seem to be most threatened when a child makes a bid for autonomy. At each stage of a child's development, the need for exploration and for testing the limits reemerges and presents a new threat to the single parent's fear of failure, or of losing the child. The child plays his or her role in this, too. Fearful of losing the surviving or custodial parent, the child will either cling or test the parent's endurance. Because these very natural emotions tend to lock the family into a tight and isolated unit, the first step must be to loosen up these ties and to involve the family with outside support. Individuals can feel easier in their relationships with each other if they feel freer to separate.

A father alone is likely to feel less competent in the nurturing role than a single mother. Our society does not prepare men appropriately, nor does it reward them. Someone is always there to say, "How can you do it?" or "Don't you need more help?" – as if to say, "It's impossible for you to be doing well." Since this echoes the single father's own fears, he is likely to feel incompetent. Then he'll either try to be perfect and deny his fears or become increasingly anxious.

There is far too little research about the effects on children of being raised by a single father. Some investigators have claimed that single fathers fare better than single mothers in their relationships with their children.* Mothers alone report more problems with their children than do fathers, though this could reflect gender differences in reporting rather than the actual number of problems. Children seem to appreciate a father's efforts, but rarely express any appreciation for mothers, as if they take nurturing from them

---

* A. M. Ambert, "Differences in Children's Behavior Toward Custodial Mothers and Custodial Fathers," *Journal of Marriage and the Family* 44:73–86 (1982).

for granted. Custodial single fathers describe greater satisfaction with their parenting role. Society, however, is likely to distrust them – to see them as potentially "footloose and fancy free." For responsible fathers like Charles, the reality is quite the opposite. Many devoted single fathers spend all their time supporting and caring for their children and ignore their own needs for adult companionship.

Successful single fathers quickly learn to do the housework, the house management that they may never have been exposed to. They are likely to be good as disciplinarians and firm in their convictions about goals for their children. Like women, they need outside supports such as day care or a supplementary person to help in the home – particularly if they are trying to manage a full-time job and the household. Men are more likely to seek such help than are women. And because the pay scale favors men, they are more likely to be able to afford it. For fathers, the major deterrent to success may be the failure of society to recognize their potential competence and to back them up for their effort. When men are already known in a community, as Charles is, their strength and determination are more likely to be recognized. Charles's competence and responsibility as a policeman were already widely appreciated.

With increasing numbers of single fathers due to divorce and a new attitude toward custody arrangements, they are more likely to be supported than looked upon as oddities.* The more able single fathers are to find a network of men in the same situation – perhaps through local chapters of Parents Without Partners or through a day care center or school parents' group – the less lonely and unusual they will feel.† Because the staff in day care and the early grades tends to be female, fathers would do well to work closely with these women to balance their own nurturing.

As is true with any single-parent situation, the children of fathers alone seem hungry for a nurturing person of the opposite

---

* B. E. Robinson and R. L. Barrett, *The Developing Father* (New York: Guilford Press, 1986).

† For information about support groups for fathers, contact the Fatherhood Project, Bank Street College of Education, 610 West 112 Street, New York, N.Y. 10025.

The Cooper Family

sex. They are likely to seek out and find female figures in their daily environment. This hunger on the part of his children makes it difficult for a father to bring home a female date. The children are likely to gobble her up or to ignore her, demonstrating their deprivation in either case. If the father should deepen his relationship or continue it for some time, the children will regard it as permanent. If the relationship ends, disappointment follows. After a few such experiences, children will cease to trust women. The children's ability to identify with and become attached to a woman may even be endangered.

A single father may find himself seeking out female relationships just for his children. It is better to do this directly – by hiring a nurturing sitter or housekeeper, full or part time, or making sure there is a female relative or teacher or day care staff member on whom the children may rely. In such a person, personality is as important as domestic skill, for the children will be looking for caring attention and an opportunity to identify and form a relationship.

Whether the mother is alive but not present, or, as in Charles's case, has died, her image should be kept alive for the children. A father must stress her good qualities, as a model, and also to balance their strong tie to him with an important female figure. No matter how angry a father may feel or how much he may blame her for deserting him and his children, it is better for the children to feel loved by their mother. This is difficult for many men after a divorce, but it is critical to a child's ultimate development of a rounded personality. Everything we know about child development points to the child's need for several opportunities for identification. Children must learn about the way both sexes react. Otherwise, they rely too heavily on the model of one parent.

Even in the case of a father who is both nurturing and firm – as Charles is – other relationships are vital. Children who live with one parent can become overly dependent on that parent. They are bound to wonder what would happen if they lost him. For the Cooper children, whose grandmother may soon enter a nursing home, this need is intensified. A girl Yolanda's age may seek out and cling to inappropriate girlfriends. Charles must help her become involved in female activities where she can find women on

Fathering Alone

whom to rely. The father of a girl approaching her teens will also worry about explaining the changes that come with puberty to his daughter. She will need both his understanding and that of a woman who can explain some of these changes with her. I recommend that girls this age and their parents read some books on female sexual development. These may answer some questions and encourage a girl to ask others. A father could help her find the answer in a book, and then use that as a springboard for more discussion of her concerns. For a girl, like Yolanda, whose mother has died, questions about a changing body will take on a greater intensity. She will need to be reassured, both by her father and by a knowledgeable woman, that her developing body is healthy and changes are normal. Making sure that a daughter can talk to a nurse or woman physician is another way to ensure support for a motherless girl.

In a family with only one parent, the oldest girl is often given heavy responsibility. It is not fair if she is the only one who helps. All children can develop a sense of responsibility for the family. A small child, boy or girl, will need more supervision and may take longer to learn how to set the table, how to clear and rinse dirty dishes, to dust or sweep. But no child should be denied the chance to contribute and the feeling of confidence that comes with helping out.

Whenever a family can participate in housework together, important bonds are formed. Make a game of it. Sing as you work. Make special stories or jokes to lighten the load. Do all you can to make housework a family project – each member contributing his or her special part. Recognition and praise for helping can be reinforced by special freedoms and trust.

In Yolanda's case, she has assumed a large part of the responsibility for Charles, Jr.'s, care in the afternoon when her father's asleep. Could she be rewarded openly for that? An allowance, not as pay for child care, but as a reward for being a responsible member of the family, would be appropriate. I would also want her to know that her help benefits her entire family. She has heard all of this already from her father. But it never hurts to repeat it over and over. A father like Charles, Sr., might see to it that his daughter has a chance to bring her friends home to a party on a few regular occasions. He could also foster her relationships with a few other girls by taking two or three of them on an excursion from time to time. Best of all, he might take his daughter out by herself for a meal or a movie.

Children of single parents will test the limits in adolescence, like any others. When trust breaks down, that parent must make time to discuss the limits. Rebellion may seem more threatening to a stressed single parent. Enlisting the child's cooperation is vital. Does she have ideas about what would help her when she feels she must break rules? Including teenagers in setting their own limits and their own form of punishment is a way of letting them know that you respect them and that you understand the pressures on them to rebel. You will still have to act to constrain them at a certain point, but then it's with their full knowledge of why you feel limits are necessary. If it is necessary to ground the child or carry out some other punishment, try to renew the trusting relationship afterward. Sometimes another adult can provide a buffer. An aunt or uncle or family friend can offer a safe place to blow off steam, or an objective reaction. Above all, when teenagers live up to your trust, make sure to let them know you noticed. The loss of a parent puts added responsibility on everyone, and words of praise lighten the load.

COMMON QUESTIONS

QUESTION   I'm not a mother. I don't look like a mother, and I will never be a mother. I'll just be the best father that I can be. Sometimes I worry, though, that my four-and-a-half-year-old daughter needs a kind of care that I can't give her? Is this true?

DR. BRAZELTON   It sounds as though you think that only women can nurture. I don't. If you love her, hug her, listen to her and are tender in caring for her physical needs, she'll feel nurtured.

Fathering Alone

Your little girl sounds lucky that you care so much and are so self-questioning.

QUESTION   Somehow, ever since my wife left, I feel cheated. Is this usual for single parents?

DR. BRAZELTON   Of course. It's very tough being a single parent. Not only are you lonely, but you worry about the child's deprivation. No single parent ever feels he or she can do enough to make a "real" family. A single father probably feels that even more. Use your extended family or friends as much as possible. Peer groups for your children are also important. The most difficult thing about being a single parent will be letting the child go. You are likely to need a mate to push you to do it and to dilute the intensity of your relationship.

QUESTION   I'm curious as to where single fathers can go to get support. The single-parent support groups I've gone to consist mostly of women. Men that I meet in the same situation tend to drift off after a while. I find myself reaching out to women rather than other men. I check out my problems as a parent with women.

DR. BRAZELTON   That's one way, but I would urge you to look for men who are in the same situation you are. Your problems are probably common ones, and it would help to share solutions. Men do tend to shy away from each other in groups. The closer they get to any intimacy, the more it threatens them. That's too bad, because the need for friendship is great.

The Cooper Family

QUESTION   I've gotten a great deal of support from women, especially one that I'm seeing now. Are some single fathers more self-motivated?

DR. BRAZELTON   Most men do question themselves and their nurturing capacity. Our own past experience with being nurtured by women makes us look to women as models of parenting, for reassurance that we are caring for our children properly.

QUESTION   When my wife died, I was overwhelmed by having to do everything. I finally decided I couldn't handle it alone, so I got a full-time, live-in housekeeper. She provided a lot of the support that was lacking. Not the emotional support, because that's what I provide, but a lot of the custodial support – taking care of the house, doing the cooking. It really took a big load off of my shoulders, and I absolutely rely on her now. I think the kids see it the same way as I do.

DR. BRAZELTON   You are lucky to be able to afford one. I'm sure that it is a tremendous relief and makes you better able to provide the emotional support. It's important to provide the kind of woman you want your children to identify with. Their hunger for a female in their lives makes them extra vulnerable. You might sit down and discuss her with them from time to time, not to criticize her or go behind her back, but to be sure that you have your finger on the pulse of your household and what she means to them.

QUESTION   During my first years as a single father, I never went out. Now that the children are older, I've started going out with women again and introducing the children to them. The problem I'm having is that with each one, the children ask me if I'm in love and whether I will ever get married. They see what's happening. They need someone. They get very close, but I'm not ready to get committed to anyone yet.

DR. BRAZELTON   Children do need exposure to the other sex, and they do need to know what real love with a woman is all about. But it won't help them develop trust in women if they have to give each one up. Can you bring a sister or other female member of your family or a stable female friend into their lives? Be sure they see her often. Being a single parent makes the extended family even more important for children.

QUESTION   My wife passed away four and a half years ago and, though it was hard at first, I've found taking care of the kids increasingly rewarding. But I still worry that they're missing something, that I don't entirely understand them.

DR. BRAZELTON   You probably feel as many men do, that women are likely to be more in touch with children's development. I don't think that has to be true, particularly if you make an effort to go to their school, to their sports events, to their class functions. And if you make time each week for each child alone, you'll have a chance to listen and be in touch.

QUESTION   After taking over with my children, I felt the way you feel after taking up an exercise or activity which you haven't done before. You use muscles you haven't used, and it hurts at

The Cooper Family

first. But if you keep doing it, the pain goes away. If I keep doing it every day, won't it become routine?

DR. BRAZELTON   That's well put. We are more flexible and resilient than we think. There's another way to look at it even more positively. We learn especially fast in a crisis, especially if we cope successfully. And the kids will learn as much as you do about mastering a stressful situation.

QUESTION   Sometimes after a long hectic period, I stop and look back and see how far we have come as a family, and I feel reassured. How can I stop feeling so anxious and full of doubt in between?

DR. BRAZELTON   Some parents keep a diary, or a calendar on which to record problems and steps toward mastering them. That helps you look back and see how much has been accomplished. You can also use such a record to alert yourself to problems. When you realize that you've been stuck on a certain issue too long, or the child is not making progress in some area, you might want to rethink what you are doing or perhaps seek help.

QUESTION   At what age can children be left alone when I go to work in the morning and come home late at night?

DR. BRAZELTON   Even though children can survive and cope by themselves at very young ages, I think it is *never* really good to leave them alone a lot or with too much responsibility. Even teenagers need to know someone else is in control, or on call. For younger children, try to arrange

Fathering Alone

for a sitter or relative to be there when they arrive home. If you do have to leave them alone, see that they know there's an adult nearby who will assume responsibility in an emergency. You can also arrange a reasonable amount of organized activity, depending on their interests. Make sure your children can reach you by phone, and call in often. Then, discuss how it's going from time to time. An empty house can be frightening at any age.

QUESTION   I find I alternate between feeling like a super-parent, or else anxious and incompetent. Is that how most single parents feel?

DR. BRAZELTON   Those contrasting feelings are two sides of the same coin. *No* parent ever feels competent. It's just easier when two parents share the same fears and incompetence. Each has the other to blame for mistakes, or to offer reassurance.

The Cooper Family Revisited

❧

When I visited Charles Cooper two years after our first meeting, I had the feeling that he was surrounded – by supportive friends and neighbors, by children sharing his burdens, and by a new woman in his life. As I arrived at their duplex apartment in a suburban housing development, all three Coopers came out to greet me. Yolanda is now fourteen, but she seems more grown up than that. She has a mature air, is buxom and pretty, with her hair done stylishly. She acted like the lady of the house, greeting me, conducting me into their neat living room. She is vivacious and thoughtful, with little hint of the rebellion Charles tells me that she is experiencing.

The room was full of family memorabilia – Charles's trophies, family photographs – as well as a large stereo and a fish tank. There were three rooms on each floor. The apartment was immaculately clean and well kept. Charles, Jr., who is now six, is a tall, handsome boy who stands straight. He teased Yolanda repeatedly to play with him while his father and I talked. The two of them romped and played like puppies – alternately affectionate and wrangling. Yolanda seemed genuinely tender with him, although I would have expected her to tire of his constant advances. I noticed that she touched and stroked him constantly when he lay his head across her lap, as if they both liked to regress to the time when he was a baby.

As we talked, I learned how much this family had been through since I saw them. "She's too old, too soon," said Charles of Yolanda. She teased her father about her boyfriends and her escapades, just as Charles, Jr., teased her. I was relieved to see how much respect Yolanda had for her father and he for her, for I knew they'd been through rough times. Charles told me of their excursion into therapy. After Yolanda had run away from home on two occasions, she had seen the guidance counselor at school, who had recommended family therapy. "We all got help after Yolanda had to run away – twice!" I asked how the therapy had helped. He said, "It helped me let go a little. That's the hardest, for me and for her. It got us time. I see kids who are on crack, and I don't want her into all of that."

Meanwhile, Yolanda is in tenth grade and seems to be doing well. She designs and makes her own skirts and jackets. She also sews from patterns and has even sold some of her work. She said, "I sew – like him." As she pointed at him, Charles said, "I've always sewed. I sew for the kids, too. I'm not a stranger to needle and thread." I was deeply appreciative that he dared to expose this other side of himself to me. "But I don't get much time now. Yolanda has to do it for all of us. She has a heroine in New York – a black model she read about who is fifty years old and sews her own clothes." Yolanda brightened. "She lives in New York. I've been there." I wasn't sure whether this was on one of her runaway trips, but she told me all about visiting Charles's sister in the Bronx. "When I graduate, I want to go to school in New York, to study fashion design." It seemed to be an issue between them, for Charles squirmed a bit in his chair.

I voiced my own concern about the kids she might have to deal with. She answered, "You do have to watch yourself in New York. One girl I knew had a baby when she was thirteen. A lot of kids there are on crack. I met a boyfriend there. He liked me a lot."

Charles grimaced. "He was too old," said Charles. "He was eighteen. Growing up I spent much time in New York. There was more security then. My uncle was a police officer, and I wanted to grow up to be one. I served four years in the Navy and am a Vietnam vet."

"You are not that large. Did that hold you back?" I asked.

"I'm gentle on the surface, but when I'm riled, up, watch out. I can take care of myself. My karate instructor was one of the best, Ron McNair, the black astronaut. I learned how to take care of myself on the street at a young age." As Charles spoke, I could hear a lifetime of experience. He was telling me how he'd learned to cope both in his job and in an unsympathetic white world.

Yolanda then spoke up. "I learned to fight like my father. I can take care of myself, too. My friends all say, 'I'm gonna get

Yolanda to fight you. She can use her fists!'" Charles said, "I tell her to walk away first, but if they want to keep on walking over you, put up a fight. Don't worry about what people say to you. How they act is the important thing. Being black, you have to learn to take a lot, but also to know when people really mean it. You have to know when to stand up for yourself and when not to. Always run from a knife."

As if to avoid a misunderstanding, Yolanda says, "I was getting too aggressive and too angry. My friends told me to stop it. I've given up fighting now, and I'm trying to straighten out. Girls fight over boys, and I was losing my friends. Now I try to talk things out. I was getting a bad reputation. Now I have crazy but fun friends. We laugh a lot instead of fighting. We go around in a crowd. We sing in a group, four girls and a boy. We sing rock and roll, have drums and a synthesizer. Someone in our group was on drugs, but we talked him out of it." Charles said, "I told Yolanda, if she got on drugs, after what I've seen, I'd probably kill her. I know she's gotta try things out, but I see too much in my job as a policeman. This is how our counselor helped us. He made me see that I was holding on too tight to Yolanda. She needed breathing space. That's where two parents might have helped." He looked up at the picture of the beautiful young woman who had been his wife. The photograph of the four of them looked down on us as we spoke.

"How are you managing now?" I asked.

"Fine, I guess," said Charles. "I seem to work it so I can look after them. They're all that matters. I patrol this neighborhood, so that I can check every hour. No one's home with them while I'm at work. My mother had a stroke, and although she recovered pretty well, she was just too much to take care of. During her last hospital stay, her physician advised that she should be admitted to a nursing home. I go to visit her nearly every day, because she knows it if I don't. But now I'm *it* around here. Yolanda has her own life, so I'm the one now to take up the slack."

Charles had realized how much responsibility he'd been placing on her before and was trying to let up on her. Yolanda's rebellion had brought this problem to a head. For a man in

Charles's position, seeing firsthand the dangers that lurk for teen-agers every day, his response showed unusual understanding and self-control.

"I make a life for myself, too," added Charles. "I have my bowling and golf. I get trophies every year. But my main job is the kids. In the morning, Yolanda fixes breakfast. Sometimes I pick them up in my patrol car and take them both off to school. When they're gone in the morning, I do the housework, buy the groceries, do the errands, go see my mother, fix tomorrow's lunch, and have a snack ready for them when they get home after school. If there's any time left in the day, I sleep before my night shift. But there's not much time. I may get three or four hours of sleep a day."

I looked around at their orderly, spotless house with awe. Everything was so carefully tended, as if there were a top-notch homemaker present. I commended him on its appearance, and he said, "I want these kids to recognize the best."

"Does Charles still cling to you?"

"No, he's great now," said Charles. "He has a buddy next door. They are together day and night. He's in first grade now. He's an athlete and very popular. I'm real proud of him. Here comes Charles's buddy's mother!"

At this point, a young white woman came in from next door. Charles introduced her as "my dear friend, Debby – who does so much for us." He explained that she cares for Charles, Jr., whenever Charles can't be home. She is separated from her husband. Her boy is Charles's age, and they are best friends. Charles, Sr., seemed to be providing her with a kind of refuge and protection, and she offered him the backup and feminine companionship he'd longed for since his wife died. They seemed to have a genuinely caring relationship. She sat close to him as we talked and added her ideas and details to statements he made. They looked at each other from time to time for confirmation. I felt the ties between them. The color issue did not seem to cloud their genuine need for each other. I was glad for Charles and felt that his lonely life seemed much brighter.

As if he captured my thoughts, Charles began to tell me about his twenty-three-foot cruiser – "worth 24 grand for 5 grand." He'd been so kind to the man who owned it that when this man died, his widow found out what Charles could afford and essentially "gave" it to him. It provided him with recreation and a sense of pride. Yolanda joined in to tell me of her excitement about having it. Charles, Jr., told me how he'd steered it. And Debby told me of the excursions the two families had taken on this dreamship. Charles calls it his "Coupe de Ville." The whole family fishes from it, or just hangs out on it. "It even has a ship-to-shore radio," said Yolanda. The boat has served a multiple purpose: re-cementing the family, bringing Debby and her son closer to them, and giving Charles a much-deserved reward for his industry and selflessness.

I asked him about the problems of being black in a largely white community. He looked first at Debby, then at his children. Then he said, "It's not easy. It kept my mother out of a nursing home for several years. I finally had to throw my weight around to get her in. If I weren't a policeman here, where everyone knows me . . ." And yet he hastened to assure me that he felt a deep sense of community in his neighborhood. Again, he looked at Debby as if to get her confirmation that their friendship was accepted by neighbors. She nodded enthusiastically. He was very proud of how much this white community had accepted him. I commented on how important this must have been as he and the two children adjusted after the tragedy of losing a wife and mother. He assured me that the neighbors all pitched in whenever he needed help. They saw to it that he wasn't lonely and had someone to call in a pinch. His role as a respected policeman was no doubt especially important in gathering this kind of support.

Charles spoke again of the benefits of the family therapy. "After Yolanda took off, we decided to get someone to help us, to guide us. And that's been a miracle."

I felt that, indeed, they had used the experience to unusual advantage. Until then, they had lived with the stress and gloom of being a one-parent family. Now, there was joy, playfulness in their relationship. Charles had a female friend, a boat, a life beyond his work. Yolanda's troubles had subsided into normal adolescent rebellion. She had experimented in some serious ways, but now she seemed to be in balance. The pressures on her to be an adult in a motherless family had abated. She seemed to feel accepted and respected for who she is, allowed to be a teenager. She was trusted

The Cooper Family Revisited

and understood by her father – rare for an adolescent. Charles, Jr., seemed as delightful and secure as he had before. He had not grown up too fast, and I was glad to see it. Charles, Sr., Yolanda, and their friends had protected him and given him a childhood. Debby must be playing a vital role in all of this, and I, too, felt grateful to her.

"You've come a long way together," I said to them all.

"I'm giving it my best shot," said Charles. "I'm doing all I can to make a family without her [he looked up at the picture of his wife]. After that, they're on their own. Let's hope they make it." Unspoken was the feeling that he'd be on his own, and that he hoped he could make it. As I left, I felt confident that the Cooper family had made it already.

The Humphreys Family

❧

CHAPTER III

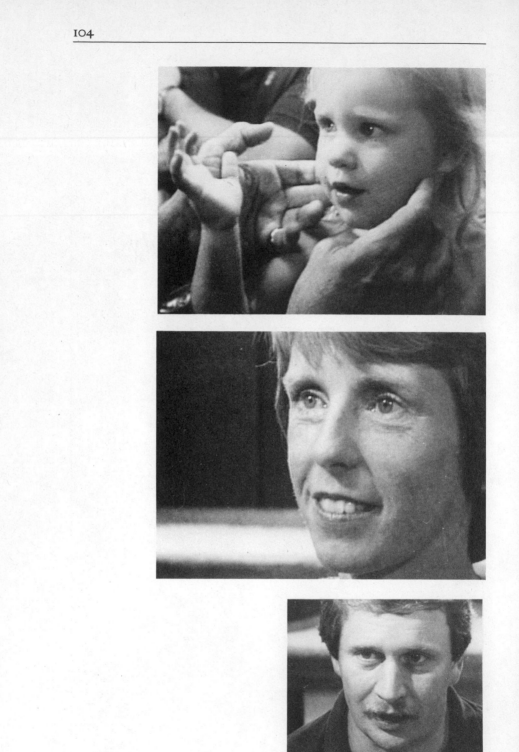

The Humphreys Family

The Humphreys Family

Family History

୬

Liz Humphreys, born in England, is a lively redhead with an ever-bubbling sense of humor. She seems constantly to be trying to make everyone around her happy. In our conversations, I began to realize that she was at her funniest when we spoke of serious matters. Though perfectly willing to face problems, she seemed to want to make them less burdensome for others. At thirty-seven, Liz is the administrator of a busy doctor's office and the mother of three children: Chris, eight; Gillian, two; and A.J., five months. Howie, Liz's second husband, works with the Environmental Protection Agency. He is squarely built – a good-looking, muscular, blond man. He exudes a sense of stolid force. No one would be likely to cross him. Genial and friendly, Howie appears in tune with all three children. During our visits, he watches each of them with pride and nods as they talk.

Chris, a lanky, brown-haired boy, was born of Liz's first marriage. He seems to worship his stepfather. He stands close to him, watching him out of the corner of his eye. While his gestures and speech have some of the flavor of his more volatile mother, there is an element of Howie there, too. I hear his identification with Howie in his speech inflections and see it in the athletic way he moves. When little Gillian comes rushing up to clasp her father's knees, Chris moves away. I couldn't tell whether he felt displaced by Gillian or whether he wanted her for himself. For he and Gillian are very close. The two-year-old trails him constantly, getting into all his belongings. Although Liz worries about sibling rivalry, I saw much tenderness between them, and caring from Chris. When Gillian was endangering a tower he had built, it was almost with pride that he said, "You *always* have to get into everything I'm doing." I felt that Liz might be reading the wrong messages into their relationship. Was she herself jealous? Chris seemed almost hungrily devoted to Gillian and to his stepfather. Perhaps this means a loss for Liz, a loss of earlier closeness with Chris.

The Humphreys Family

During our talks, the three children milled about, but Liz remained the center of attention. I asked about her background, and she told her story with great vivacity. At age eighteen, she came to this country with a teenage friend to "get away from my strict English parents." Later, she came again and stayed on to work, making herself a member of her friend's family. "They loved me and I love them. I still see my friend's mother as a second mother." Liz bounced A.J. on her knee as she told me the story of her first marriage. She left England for good at twenty-one, evading the "boring" Englishman to whom she'd gotten engaged. Five years later, she met and quickly married Chris's father. "He turned out to be a lot like my father – frightfully stiff. It never worked, and not quite two years later, after Chris was born, I just left. See how many men I've left in my lifetime? Chris and I lived on our own together for four years. It was a great four years. We were so close and free at the same time. Then, along came Howie, and we knew we needed each other. He was willing and able to take on a divorced woman and her boy. That was it."

Howie smiled. "I had an instant family, and we've had a great time. There are ups and downs but, in general, it's pretty great! I do worry about my relationship with Chris. He's such a wonderful, sensitive little boy." (He looked over at Liz, as if to say, "like her.") "I knew it was hard for him to let me come between him and his mother like I did. So I really worked hard at making him feel like I wanted to be his dad."

"After I met Howie, I realized that unless he and Chris made a relationship, there was no way we could get married," said Liz. "Chris had to be part of our relationship." When we first got together, Chris decided on his own that Howie was not going to be called Daddy – that Howie was Howie. We gave him the option, and he decided he wanted to call him Howie – "You see, because I have a real daddy." Being loyal to his dad gives Chris a sense of stability, but it also became a source of isolation in the new family. "It was going well," Howie went on, "until we started having our own children. That has certainly made it tougher on him. And maybe tougher on me. It's hard to sort out your feelings. I just can't feel the same way about each child. I'd like to. I'm always afraid Chris will feel I've deserted him, but I haven't."

Family History

Stepfamilies

OFFICE VISIT

The Humphreys family came to my office with Gillian and the baby.

DR. BRAZELTON   Hi, Humphreys family. Come in. How are you? What's on your mind?

LIZ   Well, we've got to go on vacation, and Gillian just hasn't been acting herself for the last few weeks. I don't know whether she's coming down with something or whether – you know – it could be anything else. Usually she's charging about and into all sorts of trouble, but she's sort of been just sitting around.

When a child's behavior changes, it's always a signal. In a family like the Humphreys family, for whom life is full of new beginnings, the change might have particular significance.

DR. BRAZELTON   *After looking at Gillian.* She doesn't have any fever. I can tell by the heart rate. I don't see anything wrong with her physically. Could something be bothering her?

LIZ   Maybe. Her brother Chris has been away a month with his father. She misses him and seems confused.

DR. BRAZELTON   Confused?

The Humphreys Family

LIZ   Every time he says he's going to go to see his daddy, that confuses her and she sort of mopes around for a while, so maybe that could be it.

DR. BRAZELTON   She's so volatile and so reactive. Chris is such a part of her life, such a part of the family. It's not surprising that she might be upset when he's gone.

This kind of depression is quite common, but Gillian wasn't the only one looking sad.

DR. BRAZELTON   Do you miss him, too?

HOWIE   Well, I find that this year, when he came home and said he wanted to move in with his father, we really didn't know how to feel about that.

DR. BRAZELTON   He said he wanted to move in with his own father?

HOWIE   Yes. We arranged for him to spend the month with his father, and you know, I have to feel that it's good for him – for all of us. But I had mixed feelings. I didn't really know how to deal with it. He came home loaded with presents and told us about all the ball games and parties and treats his father and step-mother had planned for him.

DR. BRAZELTON   Did you feel rejected?

HOWIE   Maybe. I just felt uncomfortable. I don't quite know what my feelings were.

DR. BRAZELTON   You know, if you feel rejected, you may be passing that feeling on to the children.

Stepfamilies

Howie's confusion, his hurt – both could affect his stepson, as well as Gillian.

HOWIE Chris is challenging us. You know, I stepped right in the middle of his life and sort of took over – in his home life, anyway. I thought I'd be his father or his father figure, and I see now that I really didn't know where I was going with it. I'm not his father and never will be.

DR. BRAZELTON *To Liz.* Do you get confused being in the middle? You know, you're almost always the fulcrum of all this –

LIZ Oh, I do, ever since the day we got married. Christopher really went through a big trauma that day. We were trying to leave to go away and he said, "I just wish it was you and my daddy getting married." And I just turned around – I guess I was tired and I'd had a long day – and I said, "Well, that's just not the way it is, and this is the way it's going to be." And I sort of felt cleansed when I said it. I thought, "Well, that's what I wanted to say – "

DR. BRAZELTON You were up against the wall –

LIZ That's right. I felt as though I had to say it, but it sounded hurtful to him. His father re-married that same month, so it was a lot for him to take.

DR. BRAZELTON You don't need to be defensive about it, nec-essarily.

LIZ That's right. But I guess that's the way I feel. *When pushed, she had been clear, but then she backed off.* I know he absolutely adores Howie – has a great deal of respect for him.

HOWIE   We've had some tough times. There have been some *specific* times – bedtime and the television have always been difficult. When I tell him it's time for bed, he just doesn't believe I've got the authority to do it. *A classic problem.*

DR. BRAZELTON   Why would an eight-year-old suddenly turn on you and say, "I want to live with my own daddy?" Could it be that you have your own boy now? Could this make Chris feel out in the cold? Whose boy is he?

HOWIE   I believe it. I believe that. *Looking down at five-month-old A.J.*

DR. BRAZELTON   Do you?

HOWIE   Yes, I think I've seen a little evidence that way. But nothing's really changed. Maybe he just feels it.

DR. BRAZELTON   This may be a very good time to sort all this out, for everybody's sake, not just for Chris but for all the family. It might be good for Gillian, too, right now.

LIZ   Would she understand? Is there any way we can explain?

DR. BRAZELTON   Explaining isn't the issue. That could be artificial. If a child lives with certain feelings, those are a lot more critical than any explanation you might give her. What she needs is for you both to be clear about your feelings. Then listen to hers. You know, Howie, if you talk about how much you longed for Chris to be really yours, even though you know he should see his own father, Chris will feel stronger. He is lucky to have a stepfather who cares that much about him. Tell that to Gillian, too. She needs to know Chris is not rejected and is not going to leave.

Chris *is* lucky. And I think he really knows it. He's loved by two families. He belongs to both.

THE ISSUES

THE CHILD WITH TWO FAMILIES. Christopher is caught in the middle — two families are part of his life. What does this mean to a child? What does he feel about being a stepchild in one family and a visitor in the other? Can he really feel that he has a territory of his own? He may feel he has to establish his identity, either by teasing Howie and Liz or by leaving them. All custodial parents go through this experience in some form. Chris's father is obviously trying to win him, too. The excursions and the indulgences are evidence of how much his father would like to give Chris the feeling that he's included in their family. But he doesn't live with them, and he isn't a real part of their family. If he were, he'd have the same problem making it with his father's new wife. Visiting for vacations doesn't give a child the necessary base for feeling at home. His father and stepmother are still on a party basis with him. He no doubt sees them as tangential to his "real" family. However, the fact that his own father cares about him and wants him to visit on a regular basis is very important. No matter how difficult the divorce and the relationship between parents, I would *always* advise that each parent be kept in as close contact with the child as is feasible. The child who sees both parents settled in new lives will find it easier to give up the fantasy that they will get back together.

The first rule in any divorce is that the child not be used as a football between two separated parents. The visitation rights

The Humphreys Family

should be clear and as well defined as they can be, so that the child can depend on the opportunity to be with each parent. In *What Every Baby Knows*, I discuss ways of making visitation, or joint custody, work.

A child's return from visiting the parent with whom he is not living will always be a hard moment. Howie and Liz are acutely aware of his father's ability to spoil Chris. He has no other children and so has time to entertain him. He has less responsibility and can play a godfather's role. Chris must flaunt this when he returns. Although he's probably doing it to test his parents, to make sure he is wanted at "home," it comes across as a painful comparison. Chris is bound to test limits when he returns. Though his own father and stepmother are strict with him, he is there for too short a time for many issues to arise. As a temporary visitor, he does not feel confined by their rules. Their main role is to make Chris happy and to have him want to come back. The contrast between this rather unreal situation and his own home, where he must fit daily into the needs and demands of four other people, makes him feel rebellious. He acts out. As Liz and Howie react to this, he either withdraws and taunts them with his other home or makes them feel guilty for holding him in. Children in this position become skilled at conveying a double message – of wounded pride and vulnerability coupled with provocative, daredevil behavior. These are universal moments in stepfamilies.

A boy who lives alone with his divorced mother needs a male figure with whom he can identify. This can dilute the intensity of his relationship with his mother. Howie came into the family at a critical time for Chris. And yet the adjustment to a stepfather, after intense closeness with a single mother, is bound to involve conflict. In an ideal world, it helps if a boy can know that his own father will stand by him as he endeavors to make it with a stepfather. The transition from being his mother's baby to forming a relationship with a new stepfather is rocky enough without a sense of having to make a choice between fathers. His own father might serve him best by standing by in a solid, caring way, as he learns to make a close relationship with Howie. But few divorced fathers are equal to playing that kind of unselfish role. Their own fears of abandonment and sense of competition stand in the way.

Stepfamilies

When a baby is born to the new family, the relationship with a stepparent is threatened again. If this is handled in an understanding way, the older child becomes able to form a strong attachment to the new half-sister or -brother, as Chris has with Gillian. He identifies with both his parents in becoming Gillian's nurturer. He may have felt shut out by her in one way, but it seems that he also sees her as his entry into the family. When I saw them together, he was proud and caring toward her. The fact that he can use her to project his feelings and fear of rejection from his family when he goes away to his other house shows that they are close. When he comes home and avoids her, while pointedly asking about the new baby, he is trying to hurt her. During Liz's last pregnancy, they formed an alliance – both positive and negative – as they both faced a new invader. In this, they are acting like a real brother and sister.

SHARING A CHILD AFTER DIVORCE. After the pain of a disrupted marriage, a caring parent will inevitably want to make it up to the children of that marriage. If she makes a second, successful one, she will see the children of the first marriage as hurt or potentially damaged. Liz had a "blissful few years" alone with Chris. She is bound to feel that she must make up to him now for what he (and she) feel as a disruption of that closeness. When he shows any pain or any rebellion, she will unavoidably take it personally. A parent who cares as she does will blame herself for all of the normal problems he would face at this age anyway. All of this is unconscious, but she will inevitably compare the present, rather thin, time, as she sees it, to the intensely close years they had together when she was single. She will remember her son as he was during this closeness and compare this memory with what he is like after she "endangered him" by remarrying and deserting him for a new family. The arrival of a new baby reminds a divorced parent of the closeness she had with her first child. If the older child acts out, either because of rivalry or because he is approaching preadolescence, her feelings of loss and guilt will intensify.

At this point, many children who live with their mothers will try to restore what they miss by turning to their own fathers. The

The Humphreys Family

reaction this evokes in their mothers is not lost on them. Feelings of jealousy and competition are inevitable in a divorced couple after a remarriage. Parents may blame their child for being "spoiled" and for bragging about what happens at the other parent's. Unconsciously, they are afraid of the competition. This blame can reinforce in the child a sense of being different, left out. The child is then likely to tease them in order to stir up strong feelings that prove to him he's really part of this family. Such teasing calls out for a firm, but loving, reaction.

A mother in Liz's position is bound to worry about losing her child, but she needn't. He needs her and his new family and is well aware of it. It is wise to avoid comparing the advantages and privileges of one family to the other. A child will know which are more real for him, but he needs both. Comparisons put a child on the spot, as if he had to make a choice. A child of divorce can never make a choice. He needs both parents, if they are available. He needs them differently, and he can sort out these differences, as long as he's not made a pawn between them.

One of the most effective ways to give a child a sense of belonging is to set firm rules and to ask him to help out in specific ways. The child will feel more a part of the family in which he plays a useful and responsible role than he will in the one that showers him with treats. The custodial family does not need to compete at this level, for the child *lives* there.

When a child returns from visiting the other parent, there are three steps his family can take to make the reentry smoother.

1. Make him feel welcome and wanted. "We want you back. You are important to each one of us. When you get back, as soon as you feel like it, give each of us a hug. We need it. We need to get back to being a whole family again. We don't feel complete when you're away."

2. Make him feel needed. "In our family, to make it work, each of us has chores to do. Yours are _____ . Your sister's are _____ , and when the baby is big enough, his will be _____ . Maybe you could teach him. He adores you so."

3. Stop talking about the child's problems. The child may

seem to enjoy stirring up the family. But such behavior labels him as an outsider. Also, in a subtle way, it can make the child identify with the failed side of the first marriage. The child who knows his family has trust in him will not need to create drama for attention and will gradually stop testing the rest of the family.

THE STEPPARENT. These days, one often hears the expression "blended" to describe families which combine children from previous marriages. Such families are very common. By 1990, more people will be part of a second marriage than a first. But the fact is, these families rarely blend completely. Children and adults with different histories and experience do not become indistinguishable from one another. They live together, but they bring the past with them. The notion that two families will become homogenized, with no more tension, is wishful thinking. The Cinderella story and the wicked stepmother in fairy tales reflect our unconscious understanding of the potential conflict. Good intentions won't make the differences disappear. However, when they are faced openly, solutions and hidden strengths can emerge. For instance, when Howie faces the fact that he had disrupted Liz and Chris's relationship, he is more able to be patient as Chris gradually accepts him. Understanding the adjustment another member of the new family is making helps reduce resentment. Nonetheless, new crises, especially around discipline, will make it necessary to face the distinction, again and again, between being a parent and being a stepparent.

Common complaints of stepparents include:

1. Lack of respect from stepchildren. At times of a showdown, stepchildren will make it clear that they do not have to obey, and do not intend to obey, a stepparent.

2. No relationship with a stepchild can feel equivalent to one with a natural child.

3. Stepparents feel that their spouses, the natural parents, do not offer backing and are overprotecting their own children, making discipline even harder.

The Humphreys Family

4. There never seems to be time to be a couple alone. When there is, couples often notice that they get along better without the children.

5. Stepparents feel they never have first priority.

6. Stepchildren act out the most after a visit with the non-custodial parent.

All these challenges of stepparenting can be seen in Howie's situation. For one, Liz is bound to be protective of Chris. He's been through so much more than the next two children. They've known only a stable family. She knows that she's put Chris through more, and she wants somehow to make up for it. While she realizes that she is making a mistake when she undermines Howie's discipline or his relationship with Chris, such a reaction seems instinctive to her.

As in many families, discipline issues began to surface only after months in the new marriage. Liz and Howie had worked very hard to introduce the marriage to Chris and to prepare him for the separation it would mean. At the time the decision was made, Howie and he were already friends. However, Chris liked Howie as a *visitor*. When it became obvious that he would be a permanent intruder, Chris's resentment began to surface.

At first, Chris had hungered for a male figure. After years with only his mother, Chris got swept off his feet by Howie. Soon, however, Howie's presence began to conflict with the universal dream: that his mother and father would be joined again. Even though each parent had a new spouse, in a five-year-old's mind, magical thinking can achieve miracles. Howie made this impossible.

At five and six, there were bound to be times when Chris needed discipline. Liz found it hard to discipline him because of her sympathy for him – uprooted and now lacking her full attention. If Howie stepped in to help discipline Chris, he was sure to get a double reaction: from Chris, "You're not my father"; from Liz, "You're so hard on him. You don't understand what he's been through." Howie would feel shut out. And Chris would get double messages at the very time when he needed a united front. I hear this all the time from stepfamilies.

Resistance to the stepfather as an appropriate authority figure is inevitable. If Liz can allow Howie to become an authority for Chris, it will strengthen their relationship. Chris needs and adores Howie, as is obvious from watching them together. If Howie can be involved in Chris's discipline, their interdependency will deepen and will become more solid. Discipline is a vital part of a parent-child relationship. The very fact that Chris must test it out whenever he returns, at a time when he is likely to feel the most insecure about his role in the Humphreys clan, attests to that.

Howie can never really treat Chris and his own children alike. For stepparents, it is a great help to realize that parents never treat their own children alike. Although they may try, it simply isn't possible. Different personalities demand different responses. These differences are magnified in a stepfamily. Stepparents are bound to wonder whether they are too harsh, discriminating against a stepchild, or too lenient. Stepchildren will naturally play on this. Howie and Liz need to continue to talk about the individual differences between Chris and Gillian and A.J., differences in ages and stages of development, differences which all of them call forth in their parents. Otherwise, at times of crisis, both Howie and Liz will continue to feel they are discriminating against Chris. If they feel it, he will, too.

The more detached and objective Howie can be, the better it will be for their relationship. But it is hard not to take acting out personally. The hunger to find a role which feels as stable with a stepchild as it is with one's blood children is common for a stepparent. When one cares as Howie does, it becomes hard to accept the role of stepfathering as a conditional one. The fact that he had no relationship with Chris for the first four years of his life will always be there. Being with a child from the first makes one feel more secure as a father. Howie can feel proud about how much Chris has learned from him and how closely identified he is with him. As Chris approaches adolescence, this closeness will need to be tested with rebellion. Howie will find this painful, unless he can see that it is based on the security that Chris has learned to feel.

The Humphreys Family

Mark Rosen, in his book *Stepfathering*.* offers important principles to help stepfamilies see beyond their own individual experience to the universal aspects of their situation. They are condensed and adapted in what follows:

1. Each child's personality and needs are unique, shaped in part by the effects of early parenting and by the effects of divorce, but also on inborn temperament. Thus, the differences between step- and biological children are not all the result of differences in parenting.

2. You are bound to react differently to each child, and the differences between step- and biological children make up only one factor.

3. Stepchildren's behavior will evolve after you are married and they are more secure.

4. Each change in your own family will both threaten and strengthen your relationship with stepchildren. It can't stay the same. Help the stepchildren to understand this, to adjust to it. They needn't like the change, but they need to understand their own reactions. A new baby, for instance, is bound to be a threat.

5. Positive feelings about your spouse will overflow into the relationship with your stepchildren.

6. Mutual support and open communication are critical for maintaining a good relationship between stepparent and stepchild. If your partner doesn't support you and disagrees about your role in his or her children's life, the chance of a good relationship is diminished significantly. He or she must back you up, particularly in disciplinary or critical issues.

7. A stepparent can alleviate problems by stepping back emotionally and defusing conflicts, rather than encouraging or perpetuating them.

8. The other parent is always a presence in the life of a stepfamily. Maintain as positive a relationship with him or her as possible.

---

* New York: Ballantine Books, 1987.

One of the most important steps that Howie and Liz could each take is to spend a special time each week with Chris, without the other children present. If each can be with him alone, he'll have a chance to continue to develop and strengthen his relationship with them and to see clearly how much a part of this family he is.

COMMON QUESTIONS

QUESTION   When my stepchildren come and go, these seem to be times of particular difficulty. Do you have any advice?

DR. BRAZELTON   Expect these times to be difficult. Each of you has to test out, once again, the relationships with each other. Prepare the children and yourself as well as you can ahead of time. Talk out the tensions openly so everyone can understand them as well as possible. Over time, you will learn from each crisis, and it will become easier. Hang on and have faith!

QUESTION   Our two newer kids seem to feel terribly bereft when the older children go and visit their other parent. I never know what to say.

DR. BRAZELTON   Prepare all the children for the separation – how they will miss each other and how they are likely to quarrel later. Ask the ones who leave to call up and touch base, or you call them. When they return, have a sort of reunion, when everyone tells what's happened during the separation. In the process, everyone can start to feel like a family again. While the others are gone, the younger children at home will feel lonely, so take them on a few special excursions to balance it out.

The Humphreys Family

QUESTION   I have a problem with my stepson when it comes to setting limits. He gets very sullen and withdrawn. It makes me angry, but I'm afraid to get angry with him. I don't know what to do in that situation. He's a teenager, and it's very hard. He won't talk back. With my own kids, I can get angry at them, because I know they still love me even if I am angry at them, but I don't know that about my stepson.

DR. BRAZELTON   This is the hardest thing about stepparent-ing – the uncertainty of the role. I'd talk to him about it. Ask his advice about how and when you can step in. Let him see that you have his welfare in mind and that you care deeply. He will be likely to respond. Letting him help you with his own limit setting lets him know you respect him. Not that it will eliminate tensions between you. It won't. Re-bellion is inevitable at his stage of develop-ment. But having talked it out gives you a firmer base for your relationship.

QUESTION   Can stepparent-stepchildren relationships ever really work out? I wonder. I hear friends who are thinking about marrying someone with children say, "Can it ever really work?"

DR. BRAZELTON   If you don't expect too much. You can never really replace their own parent. And you must learn to live with either the myth or the reality of the real parent. But you can still be a very important figure for them. They need you. And they can give you a whole new set of experiences if you can make a good relation-ship with them – somewhere between respon-sible parent and friend.

Stepfamilies

QUESTION   My husband and I seem to have different ex-
             pectations for our kids' behavior than their
             father and stepmother do. The kids point this
             out.

DR. BRAZELTON   I would make the standards for your house-
             hold clear and distinct. Let the other house-
             hold have theirs. Don't try to compete or to
             blend the two standards. Just as children learn
             to deal differently with each parent, they will
             learn to deal differently with each household.
             One of the problems is that they will con-
             stantly compare yours unfavorably with the
             other. If you can be as invulnerable as possible,
             it will defuse the comparison. But stand firm
             for your own.

QUESTION   Sometimes I see my stepdaughter's behavior
             as snotty and arrogant. Her mother calls it
             sophisticated. Do you have any suggestions?

DR. BRAZELTON   Are you and her mother getting at each other
             through her? Your disagreement is only going
             to fuel this behavior. If you disregard it when
             she's with you, she'll get the message, partic-
             ularly if you have a good relationship with her
             in the first place.

QUESTION   When my daughters look around them in the
             world, they see my ex-wife's materialistic val-
             ues being the ones that are admired, rather
             than my wife's more idealistic ones. What can
             we do to counteract this?

DR. BRAZELTON   Their mother and stepmother each have some-
             thing very different to offer them. Are you still
             competing with your ex-wife for them? That
             will do no one any good.

The Humphreys Family

QUESTION   One of my daughters cried right through our whole wedding. In her early adolescence, I was ready to throw her out of the house. But when she went off to college, she was able to write in her first letter home how much she was glad that she had two families. Her acting out was very traumatic for us, but somehow we hung in there. After she had a little independence and was separate from the household, she was able to have perspective on what it meant to her.

DR. BRAZELTON   That's what it takes – patience, flexibility, and a lot of time.

The Humphreys Family Revisited

❧

On a fine September evening, four members of the Humphreys family were waiting for me in the yard of their small home in a country village near Worcester, Massachusetts. Chris, now eleven, was out in the woods behind their house with a friend, pitching a tent for the night. Gillian, five, and A.J., two and a half, stand with their parents, reflecting their mother's coloring and their father's square build. As they came toward me, Gillian moved in a rather quick, alert way, like her lively mother. A.J. moved more slowly and firmly, like his father. Howie seems calm and confident as he watches his more active, talkative wife. He is well-built and strong. Liz seems to bounce about.

The yard is beautifully kept, with lovely rows of flowers and shrubs. There is every kind of play equipment scattered around – well-worn toys, tricycles, a basketball hoop, climbing equipment. It is a children's yard, but Liz's sure touch in the garden gives it beauty in the face of the disarray necessary with children. As we entered the house, everything was tidy and clean. The living room was out of an interior decorator's manual. I couldn't believe that it was kept like this all the time, until I looked into the "family room." There was the more appropriate chaos! It was certainly a room for all of them – with more toys, lounging chairs, piles of books, the television. It was thoroughly lived in.

Cheese and crackers were laid out for us. The children dove into the tray from time to time, but even small A.J. had a respect for the fact that this was a grown-up party. They came in to look me over, even to listen briefly, but then soon left to play together. It didn't seem necessary for them to tease us for attention. They seemed to know when they would get it and when they wouldn't. I thought I saw the reason for their clear sense of limits. Whenever they came close to intruding on our space, conversational as well as physical, Howie's firm hand or voice put a definite end to it. They respect him. They also adore him. Both children climbed up into his lap to collapse silently at one time or another. With Liz, they were occasionally more provocative, trying to interrupt as she joked and talked to me. When they were not successful, they looked briefly at Howie and subsided. He seemed a very firm anchor for these two small children.

After a while, Christopher burst into the room, grinning all over as he greeted me. He remembered our first meeting. A tall, ruddy preadolescent, he looks people squarely in the eye, while at the same time appearing to search for reassurance. His joking manner is less assured than his mother's. I could sense that he is still sorting out problems and is in a certain amount of inner turmoil. However, he is so handsome, so comfortably masculine, and so appealing, that one feels he'll work them out. He had brought his friend, a bigger eleven-year-old, who looked me over as though briefed by Chris.

"We are building a stone fireplace outside our tent," announced Chris. He appeared to know the response in advance.

"No matches," said Howie.

"We'll be careful. We've got rocks all around, so even if the grass caught fire, it can't spread."

"No matches," said Howie. Chris kept on trying to persuade Howie, who turned toward his wife, as if for support. She immediately took over and said, "Chris, Howie means it. No matches." Chris looked at me and gave up gracefully, but I had the feeling that this kind of interplay might be rather typical. Howie, who is so sure and definite with his own two children, probably seethes internally at being pushed. He then turns it over to his wife, who intercedes. I suspected that Chris did not usually let it stop there.

When I asked Howie about this later, he admitted that he still felt torn by Chris's having two fathers. He isn't ever sure whether he has the prerogative to be as firm and definite as he feels he needs to be with Chris. And yet, it was clear to me how deeply Chris needs him as a firm, sure authority. Howie is obviously devoted to Chris. Before I came, he had been out in the woods helping the boys pitch their tent. He observes Chris with a look of deep caring. He talks as though he were Chris's father. He is no outsider for Chris. But when a crisis occurs, as in this minor episode of teasing,

The Humphreys Family Revisited

a kind of basic insecurity seems to get called up in Howie which Chris senses and plays upon. I had the feeling that Howie's uncertainty makes Chris anxious, so that he keeps testing and probing. This area of uncertainty must shade their relationship.

"Chris has had a pretty tough year," said Liz. "He's had several accidents, several illnesses – a fishing hook caught in his thumb, three bee stings, two teeth extracted." Chris nodded as if he agreed. "And he's not been working very well at school, so we've gotten him to see someone for therapy." At this, Chris left the room, but remained in the next room with his friend, as if he were listening. I gathered that he was often the center of such discussions about his well-being, so I didn't try to change the subject.

"Chris is confused," said Liz. "He goes to his real father every other weekend and for a month in the summer. There he's alone with his father and stepmother. They don't have any children. So they still are able to make Chris the center of attention. They take him on all sorts of trips, which we can't afford. Then, they seem to make a point of letting us know how many things they've done for him. At least that's how it feels. Here he's just a member of the pack. We treat him as just one of us. His father has very high expectations. When he's there, Chris is supposed to behave. He comes home exhausted. He lets off steam by teasing us and kicking up a ruckus when he gets back. He takes it out on Gillian mostly. When we saw you two years ago, you told us all this would happen. When A.J. came, you said the hardest thing for her would be when Chris turned to the baby and away from her. Now when he's stressed or angry, he turns to A.J. and leaves her out. This summer, he called from his father's asking to speak to A.J., but not to Gillian. This makes Gillian very, very sad. When Chris sees that, he stirs her up, and it ends up with their being more and more competitive."

Liz's concern showed that this was Chris's surest way of getting at the whole family. "She is such an easy child. She seems so secure. I think it gets to him. He works hard to stay in charge here. Whenever she threatens that, or when she's doing something well, he starts in to haze her. None of us can stand it, so he gets a rise out of each one of us. He seems to thrive on it, and that's why we have him in therapy now. He constantly competes for Howie. He asks, 'Which one of us is better?' or 'Who do you care the most about?' How can Howie possibly answer that? At least he is very secure with Howie. He tries to be so good for his father. His father teaches him golf; they take him to drive-ins every night. We can't afford such extras for Chris. Anyway, we all do things as a family."

I wondered why Liz and Howie still seemed on the defensive with Chris's father. It seemed to me that any child would enjoy being part of their comfortable, large family.

"I think his father would like to rewrite the script," said Liz, "to be the only father for Chris. I guess it is hard for him to accept how much Howie means to Chris."

I wondered what it must mean to Chris to be fought over. When I mentioned this to Liz, she said, "I don't feel competitive, just hassled. Dr. M. [the psychiatrist for whom she works] says I feel defensive about how boring our life is compared to Chris's father's life and that I feed Chris with my competitive feelings about his father."

"Maybe Chris needs to stir up these feelings in order to get your attention away from the other two children," I suggested. "I can see that you are both so easy and secure with them."

"I've tried so hard not to get trapped in this competition. It affects Chris. He's not getting work done at school and stays in trouble. It even makes him unpopular with his classmates. He gets silly and tries to be the clown. He's having a tough time."

"I was just like him," said Howie. "I didn't apply myself and just shifted the attention from the real problem and became the class joker. I was the youngest, with two older sisters, and I was spoiled. I identify with Chris a lot – maybe too much. His annoying way of getting attention is just the way I was."

As he talked, I sensed how deeply he cared about this boy. His own past might be interfering with the ability to discipline Chris.

"Chris's psychiatrist says we should each have an hour or two with just him alone," said Liz. "We just haven't gotten around to it."

The Humphreys Family Revisited

"I agree that that's an excellent way for each of you to get close to him and let him feel it. Each of you should do it separately. In that way he can unload from time to time."

"The trouble is," said Liz, "when I pay special attention to him, he gets obnoxious, as if he were uncomfortable with just me alone. Then when he's obnoxious, I can't stand him. I even feel myself disliking him, and I hate that. He was such a good baby, a wonderful kid until he was four years old. I had him to myself until Howie and I got married, and he's been difficult ever since."

I felt that she hadn't really yet accepted the association between Chris's natural anger at her remarrying and her own guilt. She needed to work on her side of that.

Then Liz went on: "My father couldn't tolerate my getting a divorce, even though we were having a terrible time. He just said, 'Stick it out.' He was English, you know, the stiff upper lip. Now he likes Howie better, and he's glad I did it. But at the time, he really capped my divorce with an enormous sense of failure."

Liz's insight seemed to be shedding light on the source of Chris's difficult behavior. It could well have been a response to all her guilty feelings. At this point, as if to take a burden off Liz, Howie began to reveal his recent search for jobs and the turmoil he felt he had created.

"I feel like I've given Liz and her boy a rough time. I didn't really like the job I had – or I felt I was getting too old for it. I was an Environmental Protection Agency smoke tester. I had to clamber up every smokestack in this part of the country. It was exciting for a long time. But I began to see myself getting older and unable to keep it up. I left that one and for the last few years, I've been shifting from job to job. I like to think I've been learning about other career options, but I know how hard it's been on Liz and the family. We haven't any money, and we've gone on spending as if we did. Now I have a job forty-five minutes away, a steady income. It's a real relief."

Liz, in her joking way, demonstrated the tension she'd felt. "I knew he was bright but no one else seemed to notice. It took a lot of guts to go on as if nothing were happening. Dr. M. let me work overtime to tide us over the real tough spots. We had to keep up appearances in this little town. Everyone knows us too well."

The Humphreys Family

I wondered if she included her ex-husband, and maybe even Chris, as part of the audience for whom they must keep up appearances.

"We're lucky, though," Howie continued. "We have a great family. Look what we've gotten through. When we lived beyond our means, it scared me. But I wanted it for Liz. Now we've made it, and we're secure, for a change. I say to Liz, 'Enjoy it, at last!' But she's a worrier – even when things are OK."

Liz's earlier explanation seemed to fit: she feels as if she deserves to fail for being headstrong and willful, for leaving her first husband. Her fear of failure made Chris's troubles loom very large. She took them personally. The danger is that she may unconsciously reinforce him for failure. I longed to help her see that her successes were outweighing any failure she might feel. She is such a valiant, delightful woman.

Howie brought the conversation back to Chris. "I feel guilty whenever I land on Chris. I feel I'm twice as hard on him as I am on my own children, and yet the rules are the same. If I get after him for something obnoxious, I sit and worry for hours afterward."

"He's just testing you," I said. "He's manipulative. It's his age as much as anything. He needs your strong limits as well as the sense of your caring about him. That keeps coming through in everything you say."

"Oh, I care, all right," said Howie. "I feel like he's part of me, almost too much like me."

"At least from working it out with Chris you are learning a lot that will help you with your own."

"When A.J. gets stubborn, you lose your cool with him, you know," said Liz.

"But it's not the same. With A.J., I know what I'm doing."

I told Howie and Liz how glad I was that they were working on all these issues in therapy. These are universal tensions for separated families and stepfamilies. They must be aired and worked on together. When they seem to persist and rankle, it is wise to seek help. If Howie could sort out his feelings for Chris and uncover the confusing effects of the label "not mine," if he can see how powerful his identification with Chris could be if he stopped worrying about passing his failures on to him, maybe he could then relax and enjoy Chris more. As Chris moves into adolescence, the struggle will naturally become more intense. Through the struggle, Chris must become independent and yet also secure in his identification with Howie. Howie must be confident enough to tolerate it.

Although Liz says, "I've learned to stay out of it," I can't entirely believe her. Hard as she might try to be an uninvolved mother, she is part of a triangle. Chris and Howie are bound to compete for her. She will need to take Chris's failures less personally, so she can be more objectively supportive of him. Chris himself needs to learn how to succeed in important personal relationships. I hope the therapy will do that for him.

Chris is full of strength and promise. His humor and interest in others will take him far. He obviously wanted to reach out to me in spite of what might appear to be my role there – to probe his parents about him. He took me into the family room. He asked me whether I had any questions for him. I hadn't, for I felt it would have been intrusive to probe into his feelings without more to offer him in the way of a lasting relationship. I commented on how I enjoyed meeting him again. He beamed. I asked him about his summer. He mentioned visiting his father and then said, "I'm lucky to have two families. It means I get more presents, have twice as many friends – one at each house. I can have golf and fishing with my father and basketball here!"

The other two children appeared as he showed me around their playroom. They obviously look up to Chris. There's no question of their allegiance to him, nor of their feeling about his being one of them. In fact, the atmosphere in this family as a whole feels good. They are such caring, earnest people, and they are working so hard and so well on their life together. I wished that all stepfamilies could be as supportive and as determined to work things out.

As I got into my car after saying goodbye, I looked back to see Liz and Howie and Chris out shooting baskets together. They looked comfortably competitive as they played. They seemed to be well matched!

The McClay Family

Ͽ❧

CHAPTER IV

The McClay Family

The McClay Family

Family History

 za

Kevin and Valerie McClay are a hard-working couple, dedicated to each other and to their family. Kevin, thirty years old, comes from a strongly religious Irish-Catholic background and was raised in Boston with his two brothers. His father started his own oil delivery company and was successful enough to support his children through college. Kevin trained to become a police officer and got a job with the Federal Protection Safety Division. When their father became ill, Kevin and his brother began sharing the work of delivering oil after they finished their own work. More recently, Kevin has had to take on the whole service. Now he has two full-time jobs. "It does pay our bills," he says. But he works very hard and has had a particularly rough time in the past four years juggling this schedule and family demands.

Valerie, also thirty, comes from an Italian family, also religious and close-knit. Valerie has been a full-time mother for her three children. Kevin and Valerie met in their midteens at a party, became steadily attached, and married after college. Valerie's parents died while she was in her early teens. She was brought up by a sister eight years older who is still her mainstay through all of her family's crises. Whenever anything happens, Valerie turns first to her. "She never fails me," Valerie says with almost religious fervor. Both her older sisters are nurses, and she also has a younger brother to whom she is very close.

Kevin, Jr., the only boy, and highly prized as such, is a blond six-year-old, built squarely like his father. "We even throw balls just alike," Kevin, Sr., says proudly. The next two are girls. Lauren, three, is slender, with large dark eyes like her mother. She gives the impression of a good little girl who is eager to please. Dressed in a perfect outfit, she sits straight and primly, looking people over before she lets them come close. One could see that a lot is going on behind these smoldering eyes.

Stephanie, the year-old baby, is already a bombshell. She either crawls or totters toward trouble all day long. In my office, in spite of all the toys laid out for her, she made a beeline for books and file cabinets. She kept at Lauren, teasing her for a reaction, until Lauren was forced to break her cool facade and lash out at Stephanie. Valerie seemed constantly aware of the tension between these two. She could barely keep a conversation going with me, because Stephanie was so busy. I realized quickly that Stephanie kept the center of the stage by her constant, resourceful, provocative activity in the midst of this rather subdued family. Whenever they smiled, it was at Stephanie's antics. She was a constant source of stimulation and amusement. Lauren was paying a price.

In the past year, the McClay's well-ordered household had been faced with repeated tragedy. Kevin's mother, on whom they all relied, was diagnosed with breast cancer, which had spread to the lungs. Despite radiation therapy, her prognosis is not good. Kevin's father, who was deeply dependent on her, died very suddenly of a heart attack, soon after her diagnosis. "It was as if he knew he wasn't going to be able to live without my mother," said Kevin.

During this same period, Kevin, Jr., began to act tired and depleted. Even though he had always been energetic and athletic, he now didn't want to play outside, or eat, or do anything. At first, Valerie attributed it to Kevin, Sr.'s, absence. He had been away for job training in his police work for six weeks. The whole family missed him. Even after he returned, he was not around much, for he worked twelve hours a day. Kevin, Jr., would sit and mope, apparently for his absent father. When Stephanie was born, everyone else was excited. Kevin wept, saying he wanted a brother, but no one paid attention until a week later when he began to have backaches and leg aches. They were so severe that he couldn't walk. Noticing how pale and lethargic he was, Valerie took him to a doctor at the Massachusetts General Hospital. Within a week, he'd been diagnosed as having acute lymphocytic leukemia (ALL), and treatment had been started.

The whole family went into shock. "I can't even remember those times," said Valerie. "My sister had to take over. I had this tiny baby to feed and to tend to. The baby kept me in touch with reality. Otherwise, no telling what. I couldn't take any of it in. I still can't. Of course, Kevin, Sr., was the one who was hit the

Family History

hardest. He kept saying, 'I know it's my fault, somehow.' He just sat like a stone next to little Kevin. They said he had a pretty good prognosis, but we knew what cancer was and what the treatments were like. We just put all the faith we had in Dr. Truman and the team at Mass. General. So far it's paid off. We turned to our religion, and God heard us. But we were still terrified."

I asked how the other children were making out. "Lauren is the one I'm worried about," said Valerie. "She seems so worried. She overdoes it with Kevin. She's so good to him. She lets him ride right over her. She tries to be good with the baby. But every time I start to leave the house, she breaks down. She complains of headaches, leg aches. She can't let me out of her sight."

Valerie aired her many worries about Lauren and about Stephanie, who wasn't eating well. But it was difficult for me to elicit her concerns about Kevin. I respected her reasons for this; she was still grieving and too frightened to be able to face her fears about him directly. A crisis brings out many responses, and I had to respect her way of dealing with it if I was to be of any help to her and to her family.

When I first met the family, Kevin, Jr., had been treated with chemotherapy for the cancer and had been back at school for the past six months. The family had been told that ALL is the "good" kind of leukemia – the kind that can be effectively treated. Although the McClays tried to believe these encouraging words, they felt as if doom hung over them. The earlier tragedies in the family intensified this feeling. What next?

Kevin, Jr., was bloated and fattened from the steroids which were part of the chemotherapy. He had a pale, immobile face, with eyes that looked sad and staring as you talked to him. "How much does he know?" I asked Kevin, Sr., when young Kevin was elsewhere. "We don't talk about it much," said his father. "We're going to bring him up as if he were going to live to be a hundred. He's doing pretty well, too. He hasn't missed that much school. All of the nuns, his teachers, know what he's going through, but we've asked them not to talk to the other kids. We don't want him faced with it all the time. He plays second base on the Little League team, but he's pretty slow these days, and has to be careful. His whole body's so puffy. The kids think he's just getting fat, but they don't ask too much. He still does all sorts of daredevil feats on his slick red bicycle. We have to hold on to ourselves, but we let him do everything. We really don't want his life overshadowed by illness. We don't think he really knows what he's got."

This family has "circled the wagons." They have pulled back into themselves and haven't the energy to do anything else. They cling together and support each other. Fortunately, Kevin, Sr.'s, mother has lived with her own malignant illness long enough to see Kevin back in school. And Valerie's sister backs them up. The McClays' attempt to treat Kevin as normally as possible has not been without its problems. Lately, he has begun to throw tantrums at the slightest provocation. His father thinks Kevin is testing limits. He feels terrible having to discipline his son all the time, but as he puts it, "If Kevin does pull through, he'll be a monster unless I'm firm right now."

It was easy for me to support Kevin, Sr., in this decision. Although the family tried to keep to a normal routine and denied the crisis by not discussing it, there was no question in my mind but that Kevin knew what was going on. If everyone treated him with kid gloves, it would frighten him even more. After his experience with chemotherapy, fear of dying must be uppermost in his mind. When he was well, discipline for Kevin was such a normal, familiar part of his life that it must have been reassuring when his father returned to "normal" treatment.

Illness in the Family

❧

OFFICE VISIT

Kevin McClay came to my office with young Kevin, who is shy, reserved, and very brave. It is now ten months since he was diagnosed with leukemia. Though he is in remission, his puffy cheeks and tendency to tire easily are constant reminders of the ongoing chemotherapy.

DR. BRAZELTON Hello, Kev, how are you? I'm glad to see you. No shots or treatments this visit. We're just here to talk. But your father tells me that when you go to the hospital, you are very brave. For shots, you just hold your arm and don't even cry. *Kevin sits silently.* I guess you don't feel like discussing all that.

KEVIN, SR. No, Kev's a little shy.

DR. BRAZELTON There are crayons in the room out there. How about drawing while I talk to your daddy? Would you like to do that? *To Kevin, Sr.* Have you any particular questions? *Kevin went to fetch the crayons and paper.*

KEVIN, SR. Sometimes I wonder why he won't be as open with us.

Kevin's father was right to be worried. It was more than shyness. Kevin's style was to hold things in. I was concerned, too. We talked for a while until Kevin came back with a drawing.

DR. BRAZELTON Tell me about your picture, Kev.

The McClay Family

KEVIN, JR.	Those are bad cells, and Pac Man is with the good cells. And the good cells eat up all the bad cells, right?
DR. BRAZELTON	Which are the good cells and which are the bad cells?
KEVIN, JR.	Those are the bad ones.

He had a shy grin on his face, but his eyes were sad as they looked at me for reassurance.

DR. BRAZELTON	Oh, there are a *lot* of good ones, aren't there! And just a few bad ones over there? *The drawing was very simple – but it told me a lot.* Now Kev, would you go out and get me a urine sample in the bathroom. There are cups on the shelf. Can you? You go do that, and Daddy will stay here with me. Once you are done, come on back, okay? *I wanted to talk to his father alone, to hear his worries.* You say he got this idea of the good cells eating up the bad cells from someone in the hospital. To me, it's also coming from the heart. What I'm worried about is how much it costs him not to be able to ask about his fears. Just the way he does this drawing: here are mostly good cells and a few bad cells in one corner. Well, when a child talks about "good" and "bad," he can mean himself: "Am I good enough? Have I got to be good all the time?" And what I see here is a little boy who's very inhibited and very good, and who is trying very, very hard. What do you think he already knows?
KEVIN, SR.	Well, basically, just that he has this illness, and it's bad cells, and we've got to work to get rid of them, and he has to take medications.

Illness in the Family

Sometimes he gets mouth sores. You know, they're very painful, and they last three or four days, but he knows they go away – that they're only the result of medication. So he has the idea of the bad things going away. The steroids, the prednisone, make him swell up – he hates to have people see him like that. But he knows that will go away, too. He knows these are temporary things.

DR. BRAZELTON   What about the things he doesn't think are temporary?

KEVIN, SR.   About the possibility of a cure? We try to talk about that as much as possible. He knows he can lick this; we try to tell him that all the time.

He misinterpreted my question. I saw it as a kind of denial on his part.

DR. BRAZELTON   Judging from this drawing, Kevin has lots on his mind. He knows a lot more than anybody gives him credit for. I think he worries more than we know, too. Holding it all in alone is bound to inhibit him in terms of his emotional growth. It's very hard. It's painful for him, and of course, it's painful as hell for you guys. His eyes show me how much he's really thinking and how much he's – well – suffering. And your eyes show me the same thing.

KEVIN, SR.   Oh, yeah, there's worry there. There always will be.

DR. BRAZELTON   Is it too hard for you to share it with him?

The McClay Family

KEVIN, SR.   Well, we try to help him as much as possible; we want to save him as much worry as we can. *This was understandable, but not what his son was asking for.*

DR. BRAZELTON   Suppose he asked you something like, "What if the good cells aren't good enough?"

KEVIN, SR.   That's quite a question. I don't know if I would come right out and let him know the possibilities. *My question really shook him.* How could I go about it without really scaring him?

DR. BRAZELTON   Are you afraid?

KEVIN, SR.   Sure.

DR. BRAZELTON   What arc you scared of?

KEVIN, SR.   Death. *First, Kevin, Sr., had to face his own fears.*

DR. BRAZELTON   On the one hand, you know he's doing great; on the other hand, you're scared to death.

KEVIN, SR.   The unknown is what frightens you.

DR. BRAZELTON   Exactly. And you'd probably draw a drawing like this yourself, wouldn't you? You know, if you look at your fears, his fears are bound to be parallel ones. They must be. The things you're afraid of are bound to be the ones he hasn't touched on, because when you and your wife *can* talk about something, the fear goes out of it to a certain extent. *Kevin, Sr. nods.* You know, he's an amazing little boy. *There is a knock at the door.* Who's knocking? Ah, look who's here. You got through! Good boy. Come on in. *To Kevin, Sr.* I think what you two guys are doing together is really great, and I love your drawing, Kev. That's a good drawing. You're a smart boy. Now and then, you must have some questions about everything that's happened. I wish you would ask your father these things.

KEVIN, SR. So do I, Kev.

KEVIN, JR. *To Dr. Brazelton.* Want this?

DR. BRAZELTON Another drawing of yours? Oh, I'd like to have it. What is this?

KEVIN, JR. A rainbow.

He had drawn a rainbow right over the bad cells, as if to forget them.

DR. BRAZELTON It's beautiful. Thank you.

I showed the drawing to Kevin, Sr., who immediately recognized the implication of the rainbow. His face fell. He looked up at me, as if he recognized how critical it was to face Kevin's fears with him.

THE ISSUES

Every family has its own pattern for coping. After the diagnosis of a life-threatening illness, there is likely to be some degree of *shock*, of disbelief. Like Valerie, many parents can't remember the first few days. Just getting through them is a major task. There is often little energy left over for parents to help a child with his or her side of it. Being there for support through each crisis as it comes along is the best a family can do. If a child must be hospitalized, which Kevin was not, one of the parents should try to stay over with him. Fortunately, most good hospitals now encourage parents' presence and participation. They can and do sleep on a cot or in a chair next to the patient. They are taught how to give medication and certain kinds of therapy, which in turn gives the sick child the comforting feeling that his or her parents are still in control. They are encouraged to prepare a child in advance for each step in the therapy – especially the painful or intrusive procedures. Parents' active participation mitigates the fear of the unknown for the child and also helps them confront their own feelings about the child's illness.

None of this involvement comes easily. At Children's Hospital, when we urged parents to prepare small children for hospitalization and medical treatment in advance, we found that only 20 percent of parents felt that they could do this without help. Our help consisted of sitting down with them and discussing their own fears about the child's illness. Then, and only then, could they go on to prepare the child to face the separation, the fears of mutilation and pain, of strange procedures and environment. We already knew from our research and that of others that a parent's preparation of a child for hospitalization significantly reduced the child's fears and unhappiness in the hospital, significantly improved the child's actual capacity to cope with the illness and treatments, and significantly reduced serious problems at home after discharge. (Interested readers should see page 246 for addresses of helpful organizations.)

During the early days of a child's serious illness, *denial* of the life-and-death implications of the diagnosis and the possibility that the treatment might not be successful is very common. The doctor in charge of the treatment or surgery will stress the optimistic side of the prognosis. He or she is likely to be idealized as the godlike figure who is saving the child. When the child improves or goes into remission, a parent's awe and gratitude are likely to be unbounded. This positive outlook helps everyone through the first harrowing period. In Kevin's case, Dr. Truman has been optimistic all along, feeling that Kevin has a kind of leukemia which is responsive to chemotherapy. He has never openly faced the possibility of a poor outcome with the family, in part because he doesn't believe it will come to that, and in part because he feels that optimism will help them get through this major adjustment. It has. They have latched on to his hopeful prognosis and have entered the next stage of coping with a very powerful defense in place – that of denial. Denial is the most common and most powerful shield we have in dealing with a terrifying situation.

Eventually, parents must face the reality of the threat and begin to face the future. They must try to understand the diagnosis, the side effects of the treatment, and the possible outcomes. Most parents are not ready to do so right away. They keep their fears and their grieving repressed until they have recovered from the initial shock. Then any caring parent begins to feel a mixture of feelings, including *guilt*. No matter how hard he or she tries to be optimistic, fears will emerge, together with the haunting question: "What should we have done differently?" Parental guilt is not rational. It may not have any basis in reality, but it crops up over and over. Kevin, Sr., might wonder: "If only I'd not been away. If only I hadn't had two jobs." Valerie might ask herself: "What if I hadn't brought Stephanie into the world? Could I have given more to Kevin, protected him from this in any way? Was it something in his food, the water, or chemicals – or anything I might have changed that would have avoided this for him?" A parent is bound to feel responsible and to be overwhelmed with guilt.

Anger will come at some stage, too. "Why our family? Has the doctor made a mistake? Have they done enough? That nurse is so busy and so unreachable. If she'd only stop and explain everything, I could be a better support for Kevin." This, too, is a normal, healthy reaction. But it can be frightening to parents who feel close to losing control.

Guilt and anger are likely to be followed by further defenses. *Denial* will continue, denial that the treatments can be anything but successful, that anything other than complete recovery is possible. This can result in selective listening as the doctors and nurses present the facts. Parents may also avoid the questions that might lead to frightening answers. Denial is double-edged. It is keeping Kevin, Sr., and Valerie from thinking about death. But it is also keeping them from being open to Kevin's fears and the sadness under the surface of his bravery. Though it helps parents survive, denial must eventually be loosened. As I faced this with the McClays, I did not intend to rid them of necessary defenses, but to help them become aware enough to help Kevin, Jr., with his fears and to share some of them with him.

Another likely defense is *projection*. I saw little evidence of this as the McClays talked to me, but it could come up with anyone at stressful times. Parents are likely to blame others (doctors, nurses, close members of the family) for not taking enough care of their child, or for not knowing the right treatment. The tendency is to project the inevitable guilty feelings on others, especially when anything goes badly. When treatments work and all goes well, as in Kevin's case, parents are usually far too grateful to dare to criticize the medical profession. Magical thinking enters in here; parents are afraid to break their streak of luck. But when treatment fails for reasons beyond anyone's control, parents lash out, fleeing their sorrow and guilt by blaming the staff. Often members of the medical team get angry and fight back to protect themselves. I urge them to see these reactions on the parents' part as a defense against overwhelming feelings. If we can help parents see the feelings as necessary and normal, though not based on reality, they can handle their side a bit better.

Detachment from the illness or from the child can also occur in overwhelmed parents. They may not show up to stand by the sick child. They watch television in the child's room rather than paying attention to the child. Sometimes it seems too much for parents to face the pain in their own child and in the other children in the hospital. This may be a necessary defense. But it is the job of those helping parents to show them that they do have the energy and the resources to stand by and support their child.

Each of these defenses should be respected by grieving parents as well as by the professionals involved with them. I presented Kevin, Sr., with the challenge to be more open with Kevin, Jr. Had he not been ready, he couldn't have heard me. I'd have had to accept that it was too soon and he was still too raw. One strong clue came when Kevin, Sr., talked about disciplining his boy. Although the very fact of setting limits is optimistic (no one worries about spoiling a dying child), parents who are too busy denying reality and fear cannot recognize the child's need for limits. Kevin indicated that he was ready to listen to his son's needs and feelings.

A seriously ill child who can draw a picture of the "bad cells" in his body is ready to talk to his parents about those bad cells. The McClays could encourage Kevin to tell them what he felt about the bad cells – and what he feared. Even if the child instantly obliterates the threat with "good cells" (or a rainbow, as in Kevin's drawing) the opportunity is there. Not every parent will be able to make the connection, as Kevin, Sr., did, between the rainbow or other magic rescue and the suppressed fears. But with careful listening, another opportunity will soon arise.

The following rough guide to the kinds of needs and concerns a sick child will have at different ages may be useful:

0–3 YEARS	Children need parents with them for preparation, for handholding, to allow protest, for comfort, and to play it out with them later.
4–7 YEARS	Illness and painful procedures are seen as punishment. All diseases are thought to be contagious. Procedures that hurt are not considered therapeutic. Fears of separation, mutilation, and pain are strong.
8–12 YEARS	Children feel a sense of inferiority toward their healthy peers. They can't grasp the numerous variables in disease. Mood changes and other side effects are not understood as related to disease or treatment. Grasping the role of the different organ systems is still difficult.
13–18 YEARS	Concerns about body image, independence, and sexual identity predominate. The tendency to deny illness is strong. Adolescents need more information and a greater role in decision making.

The McClay Family

With these guidelines in mind, one can imagine the kinds of questions that a child might ask. For example, the following is a sampling of the kind of questions a child of four to seven years old might ask.

"WHAT HAVE I GOT? WHAT WILL THEY DO TO ME?" With direct questions like these, parents can share as much simple information as they think the child can handle. The very act of answering and of being ready to listen to questions in the first place will be reassuring. The younger the child, the more concrete the questions and the simpler the answers required. For instance, "You have a blood problem. In your blood are good cells which carry oxygen from the air you breathe all over your body. Some other cells are fighting these good cells. That's why you were pale and didn't have any energy. Remember? Now that the doctors are helping your good cells overcome the bad ones, you feel better, you have rosy cheeks again, and you have more energy to play and go to school." When the child asks questions that you cannot answer, such as "How does the treatment work?" you can say, "I don't know exactly how it does. Maybe the doctor can explain it to both of us. Let's ask her."

"I DON'T LOOK RIGHT. ALL THE KIDS TEASE ME. WHAT CAN I DO?" When a child is teased, because of baldness from the chemotherapy or puffiness from steroids, for instance, a parent must listen sympathetically. A parent might ask, "Do you want them to know that you're being treated for an illness? You could tell them, you know." If the child wants to keep the treatments private, this can be respected. The most important support a parent can offer is the time and the place to listen to the child's hurt feelings. Home must be a safe place to complain and to spill feelings.

"WHY DID I GET SICK? DID I DO SOMETHING I SHOULDN'T HAVE?" Sometimes a child in Kevin's situation will start to confess real or imagined faults and "badness" that he thinks might have caused the illness. He needs repeated reassurance. "Nothing you did made you sick. All those things are really OK, and every kid does them. I did them myself, and I didn't get sick. We just don't understand why you got sick – or why some kids do and others don't. It certainly hasn't anything to do with what you did or didn't do. But I can understand how you feel guilty. Do you know that I do, too? I wonder what I did that made you get this. And yet I know that I didn't really do anything. But all of us (Mommy, Daddy, sisters, and brothers) wish so hard that you weren't sick, that we blame ourselves. You're bound to, too, but it's not true. From now on, tell me when you have a question like that. Maybe I can help you try to answer it. I'll let you know if I can't."

"WHAT SHOULD I DO WHEN IT HURTS? I TRY HARD NOT TO CRY WHEN HE DOES ALL THOSE THINGS, BUT I CAN'T HELP CRYING WHEN IT HURTS." Children should be told that everyone, adults included, cries when there is pain. If parents allow themselves to cry occasionally, children will know it is normal and allowed.

"WHY DO YOU PUNISH ME WHEN I'M SICK?" A parent can explain that family rules still hold, illness or no illness. This will reassure the child. At the same time, the parent can make clear that being good all the time won't make the illness go away. "When you are bad, then I know you're my old Kevin. But that doesn't mean I'll let you get away with it!"

"AM I GOING TO DIE?" As long as there is any hope of recovery, parents must, and will, keep that hope alive. But they must also be honest about the severity of the disease, for the child will take in what happens to the children he sees in the hospital. In a terminally ill child, there may come a time when the child knows he is dying and the parent is certain that he knows. Then the time has come to talk openly about death.

"WHAT IS DYING? WILL I BE ALONE? WILL YOU COME THERE?" Here parents must express what they believe and acknowledge what they do not know. Most important to a child is the knowledge that, as long as he is alive, his parents will not leave him, will be there to comfort and hold him. For most children this age the main fear is that of separation. Parents can address this fear by saying, "We won't leave you; we'll stay with you all along." It is also important not to concoct a sweet, happy story which the parents do not believe. It is better to pass on deeply held beliefs or honest puzzlement. The fact that everyone dies and everyone wonders about death can be used to draw the living and dying together.

"WHAT IF THE TREATMENT STOPS WORKING?" "Then we'll face it together." A parent can point out that new treatments are discovered every day, but also that whatever happens, the family will confront it together. Referring medical questions to the doctor or nurse and encouraging the child to ask them himself makes the child feel less helpless.

To be ready to answer such questions as these and the many others that will arise, parents must allow themselves time to reflect on their own feelings and deeper beliefs. This does not come quickly. Many cannot be open with their sick child at first. A period of numbness and denial will not hurt the child. Parents must handle their side of it in order to be able to be calm and straightforward. The child will need time before he is ready to hear honest answers. At any rate, given time, the family's capacity for an open dialogue will improve. Gradually this will grow and the parents will become ready for whatever they have to face in the future. While there is no way to spare a child fear and sadness, parents can share these feelings as they arise and offer the child a constant and loving closeness as he faces what his own life holds.

COMMON QUESTIONS

QUESTION   My daughter was healthy one day, and then suddenly there she was in the hospital with bad burns. I just couldn't accept it. Do you feel that the parents have to mourn the healthy child before they can accept the sick child?

DR. BRAZELTON Yes, I do. One of the jobs that a hospital staff must assume is that of helping parents to mourn, to regress, to grieve, and then to reorganize around the real child and her illness. This is a reason for having parents stay in the hospital with a child. They can learn their new job as the child recovers and before she goes home.

QUESTION When my daughter was diagnosed as diabetic, we indulged her for quite a while. Now she expects us to take care of everything.

DR. BRAZELTON With any lifetime disease such as diabetes or asthma, the most important thing a parent can do is to pass on to the child the feeling that *she* is in control of it. As soon as she is old enough (five or six), teach her to measure her urinary sugar, to judge her dose of insulin, and eventually to give it to herself. I would help her learn to understand her body's reactions and how to control them. After each success in mastering a crisis, point out to her, "You do know how to master your diabetes." When she has been successful in controlling herself from day to day, give her the feeling that she is in charge of her disease. An asthmatic child can be taught the same kind of control. In this way, you can help her avoid the psychosomatic dangers of her disease – the feelings of invalidism, of helplessness, of being damaged or different. The sooner you as a parent can encourage independence and self-treatment, the better. It is also particularly important for a child with a chronic ailment to learn early to do household chores, to be responsible for certain parts of the family life. These bolster a sense of being a full participant. She'll grow up with a better image of herself despite her diabetes.

QUESTION   Our son is a paraplegic because of spina bifida. The issue of control is especially important. When he finally got his driver's license and could get himself in and out of the car, he really grew up and thrived. He drove before most of his friends did. The other area where he feels in control, because he has the use of his upper body, is in the water. He loves to snorkel, because he can haul himself wherever he wants to go in the water. Should we encourage him in these areas?

DR. BRAZELTON   By all means. You have certainly encouraged the right things. A child with spina bifida or cerebral palsy needs to be helped, even pushed, to feel mastery over whatever intact muscles he does have. I shall never forget the face of a three-year-old palsied child who was trying to move a heavy toy and called to me: "I *said* come here and help me. I want your help. Now get over here!" At three, with this sense of entitlement, she was on her way to a full life.

QUESTION   After our daughter's accident, people kept telling us to get back to "normal" life. But normal in a household where you have a sick child is not the same as normal in the big, wide world. All we can do, I think, is come up with a way of living that *feels* normal. It's hard. The child is growing, too, and just about the time you think you've got it, life changes again. School

Illness in the Family

or camp or dating are all a huge challenge. Will we ever be able to put one foot in front of the other in ordinary day-to-day living? We are still just getting by.

DR. BRAZELTON   Your remarks are right on target. Those of us who care for sick children and their families have to be careful not to have some standard in mind called "normal" and use it as a comparison for a family under stress. You do need to find your own level, your own sense of normal, and to value it. At each stage of recovery from the accident, your daughter must feel proud of each new level of adjustment. Your family may be just getting by right now, but it will get easier in time. It may be valuable to look back over the stages of recovery you've been through. In this way, you can recognize your successful reorganization. One very important function of support groups can be just this. In a peer group with similar problems, you can see the universality of the struggle and of the grief. Often you can see a family who has made it and overcome their difficulties. A sense of what is possible can grow from such encounters.

QUESTION   Why is someone who is dying treated like some fragile doll or saint? After we learned that my teenage nephew had cancer, immediately anything he ever did wrong was forgotten. Once when we were together, I got mad over something trifling and we had a fight. I was feeling guilty about fighting with him, but the more I felt guilty, the more I got angry and the more I fought with him. In the end, he laughed and thanked me. I asked him why, and he said, "You're treating me like I'm still alive and a person."

DR. BRAZELTON What an elegant description of a young man dealing well with his own tragedy. Treating him as a normal person gave him a chance to regain that image of himself. We do tend to isolate the dying by treating them with kid gloves. In the same way, discipline reassures a sick child. He knows all too well why you are indulgent. Setting limits and having standards for a sick child to live up to demands that they rejoin the human race. He will be grateful for it.

QUESTION Why must a parent always be honest about grim medical facts?

DR. BRAZELTON Honesty creates a basis for sharing the fears, the tensions, the anxieties which any illness creates. If a child knows (and she will) that you are lying to her, she feels she dare not trust you. Then, not only must she handle her fears and her anxieties without you, but her fantasies of what may happen are likely to be worse than the disease itself. Being left in the dark is more frightening than anything else.

A parent once told me the following story. Her son was in the hospital being treated for cancer and she was taking him out to dinner a lot. She noticed that he was getting more nervous each time. Finally he said, "Mom, is something wrong? Am I worse? You're taking me out to dinner all the time." She thought for a moment and said, "Remember last year when you played ball? They had a hot dog stand, and we used to eat hot dogs after the game. This time you're playing on a

Illness in the Family

field that doesn't have a hot dog stand – the hospital. So we're going to McDonald's instead." Because this mother had been straight with her son throughout his treatment, he was satisfied and relieved by her answer.

The McClay Family

Helping the Other Children Cope

૨ક

OFFICE VISIT

On the next visit, Valerie brought in Lauren and Stephanie. After catching me up on Kevin, she began to talk about Lauren. She was concerned about how much Kevin's illness was affecting her. Lauren is a self-contained three-year-old. She arrived wearing a frilly dress, her hair curled. She looked around to be sure she was pleasing us – the picture of a good little girl. She dutifully put out her hand to greet me.

VALERIE
Lauren and Kevin had the usual sibling rivalries, but when Kevin got sick, she started catering to him. She gave in to his every little wish. Even at two and a half, she was aware of what he was going through. Whenever he asked for something, she'd run and get it.

DR. BRAZELTON
Did this come from imitating you guys?

VALERIE
Yes, it probably did. But just a little while ago, she began to change and get tough with him again.

DR. BRAZELTON
And what happened? Give me some sort of sequence.

VALERIE
As Kevin started to look better and feel better and act better, she decided, "Wait a minute, no more of this." Because he was also taking advantage of her.

DR. BRAZELTON
When did she turn?

VALERIE   Just recently. Not until he was better.

DR. BRAZELTON   *To Lauren, whom Stephanie was pummeling.*
                  Goodness sakes! Look at that baby! She really
                  hurts you, Lauren. That's better! Fight her
                  back! She doesn't have to hurt you!

Lauren was fighting back – a very healthy sign. But the way she did it concerned me a bit. Her aggression and her anger were near the surface, but she couldn't really let herself go. I wanted to talk to her mother about what was behind this, so I suggested to Lauren that she find herself some toys in my waiting room and take Stephanie with her.

DR. BRAZELTON   I didn't really want to talk in front of them,
                  because I think they have been through so
                  much and understand so much. You know,
                  when a family's under too much stress, chil-
                  dren hold back their grief and their own con-
                  cerns. When everyone gets back in balance,
                  then they unleash their reaction. That's when
                  they get angry. This ability to save up feelings
                  until everyone can take it again is really rather
                  marvelous. Now Lauren seems to be letting
                  go with Kevin. But she is still trying to be too
                  good with Stephanie. She really takes a beating
                  from her. She could be building up a lot of
                  anger at that baby – when the baby's kicking
                  her and pulling at her face.

VALERIE   Yesterday, as a matter of fact, Stephanie had a
                  piece of meat in her mouth and was crawling
                  around with it, and Lauren tried to get it out
                  of her mouth, and Stephanie bit her finger.
                  Then she went over to Stephanie and hit her.
                  She actually gave her a good smack.

DR. BRAZELTON   What did you do?

The McClay Family

VALERIE   I just told her not to hit Stephanie.

DR. BRAZELTON   How did you say it?

VALERIE   In a nice way.

DR. BRAZELTON   Maybe you're too nice. You have to learn to be more open, too.

VALERIE   I often wonder – how far do I let them go?

DR. BRAZELTON   Before you step in?

VALERIE   Yes.

DR. BRAZELTON   When do you generally intervene?

VALERIE   Well, I let them go for a little while, but when they really start pulling hair or whacking each other, then I will step in.

DR. BRAZELTON   What happens if you don't?

VALERIE   Well, one will come crying to me, "She just hit me."

DR. BRAZELTON   So, they draw you into a triangle; they make a triangle with you whether you like it or not. *This is a classic conflict. Valerie was unwilling to discipline, yet unable to let them work it out themselves.*

VALERIE   But what can I do? Do I say right off the bat: settle it yourselves?

DR. BRAZELTON   Could you?

VALERIE   Well, I'd have to work at it. It'd be hard –

Helping the Other Children Cope

DR. BRAZELTON   I think so, too. *It will be, until she can see what is happening.* Valerie, you described their running back to you, as if that was some sort of safeguard against their hurting each other. Do you feel that as long as you're there and they're running to you, that they're safe?

VALERIE   Mmmm mmmm. Yes, actually . . . *She was beginning to see that she was being too protective.* But when do I step in?

DR. BRAZELTON   Maybe you never need to, as long as they're running in and out like this, because what you're saying to me is that as long as they're running in to you, you feel comfortable.

VALERIE   But I want them to stop. *Her children were giving her the answer.*

DR. BRAZELTON   Are you afraid of letting go yourself?

VALERIE   I guess I'm still too tense from Kevin's trouble. I just can't deal with any more upset, any more anger or fighting. How *am* I going to deal with it?

DR. BRAZELTON   You know, I've noticed one thing today – how close you are together – how you cling to each other almost in a group, as if you were protecting yourselves from what all of you must be afraid of. You're holding yourselves in, setting limits on everybody's relationships, everybody's acting out. This is good, temporarily. But it won't last. The next stage – which is

The McClay Family

really what you are asking me about – is giving the kids a chance to work out some of these feelings.

THE ISSUES

I am pushing Valerie to see the girls' side of this adjustment. She may not be ready yet to hear me. As she says, she's been through too much lately to take any more chances. How could she live with herself if she let Stephanie or Lauren hurt one another? She has too many guilt feelings threatening her, as it is. For parents who have been through a dire crisis, any anger or any show of negative feelings on the children's part brings some pretty strong emotions to the surface. These raw feelings are barely submerged, barely held in check, and parents are afraid of losing control.

When a child is very sick, everyone in the family is bound to suffer. Parents wish they could spare the other children, and they try to. But it's impossible. The other children pick up the parents' anxiety. They become afraid and try not to upset the delicate balance which they can sense. It always amazes me that children can be so sensitive to their parents' reduced tolerance and can save their own reaction until the atmosphere feels safer. But if this goes on too long, it can be expensive for the child's total development. Lauren, apparently an outgoing, happy child, changed to a quiet, repressed one – all too sensitive and eager to please. She becomes frantic when her mother leaves the house. These fears of being deserted, of losing someone else, are very common among the siblings of critically ill children.

For a child of three to feel responsible for the family's misery is an amazingly sensitive and precocious reaction. It means that she senses the tension the family is under and that she dare not test the system. Having just finished the provocative third year, this little girl, who was described by her parents as "something of a hellion before," has undergone a complete transformation. One wonders whether she has indeed been able to work out her negativism and her need to be provocative, or whether she feels she must repress it all. She has no outlet in being bad; she cannot

Helping the Other Children Cope

compete with her frail brother for some of their parents' concern and attention.

In a family like the McClays, I feel relieved when the other siblings start to be demanding, even bad, when they try out their wings again. At the point where they can fight, the family may be on the road to recovery. As long as parents try to keep the lid on, the children will be afraid of losing control, afraid that they might bring more trouble down on the house.

A baby or a toddler in a stressed family will reflect the tension in her own way. Stephanie, who hasn't gotten enough from Valerie through this bad year, responded with her single-minded focus on Valerie. No matter where she was in the room, her antennae were in contact with Valerie's every move. When Valerie's face saddened at one very poignant moment, Stephanie darted across the room to look up into Valerie's face, as if to say, "It's all right." I have seen this kind of role reversal, of the baby mothering the mother, in other situations where the mother is depressed. Valerie handles her feelings so well that it came as a surprise to see Stephanie's concern. I don't think it hurts a toddler to be so sensitive to a mother's pain and so protective of her, but it does demonstrate a kind of social precocity. This is the toddler's contribution to the family's coping system. I find it beautiful and remarkable.

The child, like Lauren, who is neither the sick one nor a baby may suffer from these inhibitions the most. She is squeezed between a sick brother who is on everyone's mind, and an openly aggressive, provocative, one-year-old sister. In times of tragedy, babies and toddlers are not expected to "behave," and they learn quickly how to hold the distracted parents' attention. But an older child, made quiet by a tense atmosphere, holds back. Negative, angry feelings build up inside.

Parents can help the sibling of a sick child first of all by sharing with her some understanding of what they've all been through. By doing this, they are saying implicitly, "We are through it now, and we can take your being yourself again." They can also address the issue openly. "Do you feel you don't dare tease Kevin for fear you'll hurt him? He's not that fragile anymore," or "Do you feel it was your fault that Kevin got sick? It's not at all, you know. You don't make people sick by getting mad at them. You can get mad at him now and at me and Dad. You don't need to hurt each other, and I won't let you, but you can surely get mad."

Parents of a sick child or one who has died may also have to help the siblings with fears of separation. They will need to uncover whatever is behind it. For young children, death is equivalent to separation. Also, with one child in the hospital, the other children are often separated from their parents. This stirs up additional anxiety. Even when they are at home, parents can be withdrawn and inaccessible. Renewed attention from parents helps children uncover their feelings about all these losses. Whether they can express their concerns or not, one-to-one closeness with parents will cement frayed relationships.

COMMON QUESTIONS

QUESTION   Our son was injured in a skiing accident and became paralyzed. It was a very sudden event. I'm a physician. Within two hours of the accident, my immediate boss at the hospital said to me, "Your life will never be the same, but we will help you cope." That may sound like a very harsh statement, but it was very helpful for me to understand immediately that things would not go back to the way they were. Would you recommend this kind of blunt honesty?

DR. BRAZELTON   When offered by a close, caring associate, such honesty can be truly helpful, even when it's acutely painful.

QUESTION   After our daughter's illness and death, I wrote down how I felt. I kept a little diary of day-by-day, thinking that later on I could look back at this and learn something. Isn't keeping a diary one way of recognizing how we recover from tragedy?

DR. BRAZELTON   Yes, it is. Not only can writing in it be a kind of catharsis, but you can look back from time to time to see how far you've come.

QUESTION   I'm worried about our older son. His brother has cystic fibrosis and his care takes a lot of our time. This has gone on for six years, but I still wonder whether we are asking too much of the healthy one. He had to mature a lot faster than his contemporaries. He's been an extremely big help. We've given him a lot of responsibility, and he's been able to take it. Just for medical emergencies, we taught him to drive when he was thirteen, which isn't legal, but if something happened, he could drive. Do you think he has missed out on his childhood?

DR. BRAZELTON   He may have gained as much as he gave up. I am impressed with the strengths a child in this situation develops for the future. He is likely to be invulnerable to the attractions of drugs and other acting out that his peers will not be able to resist. He must be proud of his role in helping the family cope. That doesn't mean he won't have to bitch about it from time to time, and to criticize you for making him take so much responsibility. I'd be glad if he did. But you can be confident that you've given him an opportunity to develop a firm sense of himself, including the sense of his own importance as responsible to others less fortunate. I wish that more parents expected and encouraged this response from siblings when one is in difficulty. As long as you are sensitive to his concerns and make sure he has time with you and time for friends, it's fine to expect him to help. Try to feel secure that it will pay off for him in the long run.

QUESTION My four-year-old lost her older sister. How can I tell what she is really thinking about and if she actually understands what happened to her sister?

DR. BRAZELTON Only through patience and sensitive listening. Be alert to the feelings we described earlier: feelings of guilt, of responsibility for the sibling's illness, of desertion by grieving and busy parents, of anger at "Why us?" With time together, week by week, you can gradually convey the message that it's OK to tell you how she feels. Then listen. Don't tell her what to think. You may be surprised and even hurt at what she says. But if you cut her off, or talk too much, you'll lose the chance to hear and explore her reactions.

QUESTION How can we keep our son from feeling guilty about his brother's accident?

DR. BRAZELTON You can't. A child is *always* going to feel, irrationally but inevitably, responsible for what's happened to his sibling. You can expect this reaction and gradually help him to see that it is not his fault.

QUESTION My older daughter has diabetes. When we first discovered it, we were at the pediatrician's with both girls, who were feeling sick. It turned out that the younger one was fine, but her sister had diabetes. They always fought a lot, and she would often wish horrible things would happen to her sister. A year later, she still seems to feel guilty. Even though I've brought it up thousands of times, she won't talk about the guilt she was feeling.

DR. BRAZELTON   Perhaps you expected her to unload before she was ready. You must respect a child's timing, and then, listen. Maybe by telling her she might feel guilty, you kept her from expressing herself.

QUESTION   Last February, my wife and I lost our first child. We chose this year not to celebrate Christmas, and we went away together. We ran into a lot of resentment and a lot of hostility from family members who basically felt we were sticking our heads in the sand. They also keep encouraging us to have another baby. How can we explain that we are not ready?

DR. BRAZELTON   It's their problem. They are obviously eager to help you and are feeling sad that you're not over your grieving. But you're not. It's your timing that matters, not theirs. I'm glad you aren't rushing to replace the lost child right away. If you did before you had resolved your grief successfully, you'd be likely to put a great burden on your next child, hovering and worrying excessively. We call this a "replacement child syndrome," and it is a genuine risk for bereaved parents. So, recover at your *own* speed, and postpone the next pregnancy until you have recovered. Then, it can be the joyous occasion you both deserve. You'll still be worried and tend to hover, but you'll be much more likely to have control over your reactions.

The McClay Family

QUESTION   Why should parents think of their own grief
first after a child dies? As a parent and as an
adult, I feel I should put my own problems
on hold and help the other children. Because
I'm a more mature person, I have the resources
to do that, and I don't think the child does.

DR. BRAZELTON   The reason you must face your own grief first
is that otherwise you can't really understand
what the child is going through. Parents must
get past their shock and numbness and denial
before they can help their other children. Even
if you have to repair mistakes or missed opportunities, you will be much more capable of
listening to your children and helping them.

The McClay Family Revisited

❧

The McClays live in a compact, unpretentious house in a working-class neighborhood on a dead-end street full of children. Kevin, Sr., delivers oil to hundreds of homes all over Boston. For a long time, in order to pay for their house and to get his finances off the ground, he kept his other job as a police officer for the federal government. He enjoyed the feeling of "burning the candle at both ends," working with people in his government job during the day and working alone delivering oil in the early morning and in the evening. He has two older brothers, but neither of them wanted the oil business – "It's pretty dirty." Kevin gave up the police job temporarily after his son became ill and he was needed at home. His father died about this time, too, and he was needed all the more in the oil business. "It's hard, but I'm doing well. I'm about to buy another small business, and then we can move to a bigger house. The kids don't want to, though. They love it here on this street – there are twelve kids near us who are all their ages." Kevin, Sr.'s, face softens and he grins as he talks about his family. He is obviously a soft touch for his children, but he can also toughen up when they cross a certain line, and they know it. I see him as a man with strong convictions and high ideals, who expects his children to live up to them, as he has.

When I arrived, I went to a house nearby by mistake. There were toys, cartons, and cans all over the yard and porch. Obviously, a busy family with children lived there, but it did not seem to be the McClays' style. I was relieved when I was told that the McClays lived down the street. Their five-room, two-story house is cheerful and well kept. While I was there, the children made themselves a snack. They clearly had the freedom of the kitchen and created a certain amount of chaos that I could see from my chair in the living room. But they cleaned it up without prompting. They seemed used to responsibility and to managing in an orderly way. Even Stephanie, now age four, scrambled around to help. Lauren, now six and a half, is the one in charge, and she seems to mother both Stephanie and Kevin, Jr., who is nine.

Lauren is now bright-eyed, vigorous, and on top of everything. Her mothering has taken the place of her earlier reserve and inhibition. Although Valerie complains about how much the children bicker and fight, I saw very little competition and much sharing and helpful attention to each other. "I don't pay attention to their fights," Valerie tells me. "I let them deal with them. I only go when they shed blood." I was glad to see that the tension surrounding Kevin's illness had let up enough so that she could leave the struggles to the children as much as possible. The three children appeared to be a close unit. Lauren was in the center, ordering the others around and mothering them.

Valerie is expecting a new baby in four months. Kevin, Jr., wants a boy "to balance the family." Lauren wants a girl (perhaps so that the situation won't be like the one with Kevin). Stephanie just grins when anyone talks about the baby. So far, the reality hasn't hit her. I think she still sees herself as the baby and takes any mention of babies personally. As Kevin, Sr., and Valerie talked, I felt that they saw this baby as a reward for having survived all the tragedies of the last three years – Kevin's mother's and father's deaths and the most terrible one, that of facing cancer in their own six-year-old child. The new baby is almost like their insurance against "What next?" It is characteristic of this family to submerge tragedy in positive steps toward the future.

Kevin was my real surprise. In three years, he had been transformed. When I last saw him, he was still being treated with large doses of steroids for his cancer. At that time, he had squirrel-like cheeks, a rather fat body, and the dull eyes of a child who is depressed and miserable. With acute leukemia, there is no physical pain, but there are feelings of low energy and of dread, and no appetite. When Kevin burst into the McClays' living room, I could not believe my eyes. Now he is a handsome, blond boy with chiseled features and the flushed cheeks of health and exercise. As he came panting into the room, having been "biking around the neighborhood," this nine-year-old boy glowed with vitality. He is sturdy in his build, and one can predict that he will be an athlete and a popular, outgoing young man.

The McClay Family Revisited

Soon afterward, Lauren and Stephanie followed, out of breath. All three of them greeted me warmly. I asked them whether they remembered their visits to my office. Kevin's face became serious and his eyes darkened as he said, "Yes, I remember." He sat down on the floor across from me as we talked, as if our meeting were too serious to stand up for. His deep-set blue eyes reflected the emotions he felt as he recalled our experience together. They alternately darkened and brightened and expressed the feelings that he found impossible to put into words. In his eyes, I found what was missing in his monosyllabic answers.

"Do you remember what we talked about in my office?" I asked.

"Nope." Kevin looked at me as if searching for memories which were too painful to bring back easily.

"You remember that you were worried about being fat?"

Kevin nodded. "I felt funny," he said.

"Funny?"

"Yes, about looking like a girl." Kevin looked over at his pregnant mother.

"Are girls fat?" I asked. He nodded. "Didn't the kids know why you were fat?"

"You mean my leukemia?" he said. "I didn't talk about it. They didn't want to hear about it. Kids don't like sick kids." His eyes grew very dark, and he looked down at his feet.

"So you felt like you couldn't really let them know why you were fat?" I continued.

At this point, his father stepped in, as if to protect Kevin. "When we heard they were teasing him, we went to the nuns to tell them. Before that, we'd asked them not to say anything. But now he's fine, anyway. Four years and he's got the slimmest record of anyone in the cancer clinic. When we go to the Massachusetts General Hospital for his checkup, all the nurses say, 'Here he comes, the slimmest file we have.' We can spot his file a mile away, it's so slim. All the other kids have thick files – complications, you know. He's a hero at the clinic, because he's doing so well. Now Kevin can do everything – *everything*."

While he had been in treatment, Kevin couldn't play any contact sports, nor could he do anything which might make him bleed, for one of the symptoms of leukemia is a tendency to bruise easily and to hemorrhage. At the age of six, these restrictions were probably more terrible than anything else for a boy who had been active previously. Now Kevin assured me he couldn't remember the bleeding, nor could he remember not being able to play sports. To me, this was evidence that the experience had been very painful for him – so painful that he must repress it.

"Now I can play football, hockey," he said. "I have a stunt-board, too."

His father grinned: *"Everything,"* he said again.

"So, all your bleeding is gone!" He nodded vigorously. Then I asked, "Do you remember the drawing you did in my office – of the blood cells being eaten by the Pac Man cells?"

"Nope." Kevin's eyes told me differently.

I described the drawing to him of the bad cells eating all the good ones.

"I remember drawing a rainbow," he said.

"I remember that, too."

"The good cells ate the bad cells."

"Was that why the cells were fat?

At this point Kevin, Sr., interjected: "We learned so much from talking with you. When you showed me Kevin's drawings of the Pac Man cells and, then, of the rainbow covering their battle, I realized how hard Kevin was working to make it all seem to be OK. Now it finally is OK, for sure. The clinic says he's one of their miracles."

I could see how difficult it still was for them, as for any family, to face this dreadful disease. Every time we talk of anything gloomy, there is a need to change the subject to something upbeat or positive. One can feel the importance of this defense as the parents support each other and their son in the life-and-death struggle. The strength and power of such defenses and the necessity of denial had never been as clear to me before as it was when I spoke to the McClays.

In this follow-up visit, however, I was struck with how much more openly they talked about everything in front of all three children. There was no attempt to send them out of the room as we talked of leukemia, of chemotherapy, of remis-

The McClay Family Revisited

sions. Kevin was never out of earshot for long, although he was summoned several times to come out and play by his many friends outside. Talking openly now seemed to come more easily to this family.

We spoke of the other deaths they'd experienced around the time of Kevin's illness. Kevin, Sr.'s, mother, who had developed cancer one year before Kevin's diagnosis, had outlived her husband and survived to see Kevin "through his cancer." Her husband, about whom they all worried, was the weaker member of the family. He had chronic heart trouble (they told me), and his wife worried about dying first. When he suddenly had a fatal heart attack, she said, "Now it's OK for me to go join him," and she "let herself die within months afterward." These repeated losses had accompanied Kevin's diagnosis and early treatment. Kevin was very close to his grandmother and had wept for days after he saw her on a respirator just before she died.

As his parents remembered this, Kevin asked me, "What happens when they open your heart? How do you breathe?"

"They give you oxygen by tubes just like your grandma's, and the tubes breathe for you through the operation. When you wake up, you're breathing again. Have you gotten interested in medicine since you had all of these experiences?"

Kevin shook his head no, while saying yes with his eyes as he watched me intently.

Both of Kevin's parents picked up on this. "We have talked to him about this. He's so lucky that he really should use what he's learned to help other people." Kevin squirmed a bit uneasily but kept watching me.

"Kevin, this is probably a silly question," I said, "but have you learned anything from all this ordeal?"

"Well," he said, "I don't laugh at other people."

I asked whether he meant people with something wrong. He nodded and said, "I know how they feel." I couldn't help but add, "And the next step is to want to help them." He smiled almost imperceptibly.

At that point, both parents began talking about Dr. Truman. They said he was straight-shooting from the first, never mincing words about the seriousness of Kevin's leukemia, but he also gave them hope. "There are two kinds of leukemia – the good kind and the bad kind. Yours is the good kind."

"It was the longest day of our life," said Kevin, Sr., and sighed. "Neither one of us could even take it in. We just lived through it. We were in shock. All you can do then is keep breathing. I don't know what kept us going. When we went to my mother's house – she was dying herself, you know – we both broke down and sobbed and sobbed. My father couldn't stand it. He just walked out of the room. He died a month later of his heart attack. Dr. Truman told us, 'We'll do it,' and we believed him. 'If we have one remission, we'll be on our way. After a remission, there are bound to be relapses, but we can treat them, too. We just don't know how many, and how long we have to fight it. But we can do it.'"

Kevin mentioned that Dr. Truman talked to him as if he were a grown-up.

I turned to Kevin. "If you had a chance to talk to other kids who have to face a disease like leukemia, what would you say?"

"It hurts," said Kevin. "Those needles, I mean. Especially the spinal needles."

His mother stepped in to point out that he was talking about the bone marrow needles. He nodded. But I felt he was also talking about another, deeper hurt – the seriousness of his disease and his fears about it.

"Would you want people to tell the kids what they had?" I asked.

"Oh, yes! It's important for kids to know. Anyway, I'd tell them just to get it over with. It won't last forever."

"Did you ever wonder what people were talking about when they said you had a serious disease?"

"I knew," Kevin replied.

"You knew what?"

"That I might die."

"What did death mean to you? What would you tell other kids that had to face it?"

"That even if you did die, you'd still be happy up there."

"Where did you learn that?" I asked.

The McClay Family Revisited

"When my grandmother died," Kevin replied, "she looked so peaceful and happy. She'd been hurting before. Now she wasn't. My aunt told me she'd be happy for the rest of her life."

His parents then remarked upon how long it had taken for Kevin to open up to them. They'd really worked on it, because they realized how much he kept inside. "If I'd known how important that was," said Kevin, Sr., "I'd have been more honest with him sooner. I'd have done better by him." He looked over at his handsome, sturdy son as if Kevin were the most precious thing in his life.

"It seems to me that you've done very well by him," I said. "You're so close." Kevin, Sr., nodded. "But maybe you feel as if you wish you could have spared him the illness entirely."

His eyes filled. "We don't dare think like that. We just face it as it comes."

I asked how they had managed to get through it all. They both talked of how important their families had been. Mrs. McClay's two sisters, who are both nurses, just took over and backed them up at every turn. Her oldest sister was the mainstay. This sister, who had always been a mother to Valerie, is now getting a Ph.D. in nursing. She has been a major support for all the McClays. "We all feel she's number one! I don't know what we'd have done without our families." Kevin's two brothers and her two sisters and brother have all stood by them. We talked of what a cushion it was to have an extended family, as you tried to handle such serious losses.

"The other thing that helped us is our religion," said Kevin, Sr. "We really turned to it when Kevin was sick. We both believe in God's mercy and in an afterlife. We feel our parents are right up there, and if we have to give Kevin up, he'll go to them." They looked at him tenderly, and he flushed. "The other thing is that we feel God can make miracles, and Kevin's recovery is one of them."

"Do you believe in miracles?"

All three nodded vigorously.

"What we believe," said Valerie, "is that if you truly turn to God, He'll answer you. We were desperate, and we felt He answered."

The McClay Family

"It's not just going to Mass," said her husband. "We don't always do that. We turned to Him and turned ourselves over to His mercy."

"I guess I've never quite experienced that kind of answer," I said, "but it sounds very powerful to me. What did it feel like for you, Kevin?"

"I just waited and waited – until it was over."

"No one else knew what we were really going through," said his father. "Finally, we got into a group of twelve other parents who were facing ALL. *They* all knew. They were in it, too. And we all faced it together. I would surely tell anyone in the same trouble to get into a group. It was lifesaving for us to be with other people who *really* understood."

All three then began to talk about the children they'd known who'd since died. They even referred to some children as the "bald" ones. They were remarkably open with each other, and it seemed to me like a great accomplishment to be discussing leukemia in such an honest way.

"At first, I never could quite know what Kevin was feeling," said his father. "Then I realized he would let me know he was suffering by taking it out on his sisters, or by kicking the door or the furniture. I realized that was his way of blowing off steam. And then I'd keep pushing him until he told me what was bothering him. One day he was being surly and angry. It came out that the kids in day camp had been teasing him: 'Fat boy! Fat boy!' I wanted to fight them for him, but it was too late. Camp was over. I told him it was just the medicine, not him, but I could see that it was more than being fat. He was angry over being sick. So was I. And it helped him to get it out. So we went to work to get him to talk to us more."

Kevin, Sr., mentioned how he'd begun to teach Kevin to fight back, not just to take it. "I even pushed him to fight the kid next door who's two years older. I said even if you lose, you'll be better off fighting. Later I heard them pounding away on each other. Kevin came in bruised and scratched, but he'd done it. That kid has respected Kevin ever since."

Valerie nodded and entered into our conversation. "Learning to fight things can make you a winner. I want him to learn two things from this – to fight for himself and to respect others who have trouble. Kevin has learned them both. When he hears a crippled neighbor calling his niece down the street, Kevin goes to get her for him, so he won't have to chase her with his crippled leg. I think Kevin knows what it's like, and I'm proud of him. I tell him, 'God spared you for something.'"

I mentioned that there might still be a lot of pressure on him. They agreed and began to tell me (asking my advice, I thought) about Kevin's problems in school. He goes to a parochial school and did fine the first year after his illness. "He had a sympathetic sister then." But after he began to get better, they asked the nuns not to make a special case of him any longer. "And they haven't. It's almost as if they've gone the other way. They really don't give him any room. They're constantly complaining about his day-dreaming and lack of attention. He does very well in school but they seem to want him to do better and better. They seem to think he's being bad when he can't pay attention."

"What do you think?" I asked.

"I wish he'd learn to pay attention and not get himself in trouble," Valerie replied. "Maybe he's got too much to think about, football and hockey, I mean. I want to stand up for him with the sisters, but I know it would only make it worse. You have to learn to live with them, I tell him."

Kevin spoke up. "When I don't get my work done, she says, 'Do it faster.' When I do it faster, she says, 'You did it too fast.' Nuns don't really think about you."

"And what you've been through," I add.

He nods. His father went on. "He's a class leader. They all like him and look up to him. But I guess he still does a lot of worrying. He had some therapy with a psychologist when he felt low. The psychologist said we could help him best by getting him to open up and share things with us. We're working on it, aren't we, Kevin!"

Kevin looked as if he wasn't quite sure what this meant, but I sensed in him a real desire to please these devoted parents. His expression was bright and eager, even when his eyes grew sad. There was still a lot of unresolved conflict in this sturdy little boy.

The McClay Family

How could he help being confused after the period of constant, overwhelming attention to his illness and the deep sadness of everyone around him? Whatever his understanding of all this might have been, he's bound to have shared and sensed his parents' anguish. I could sense a special kind of closeness between father and son, as if the strength of their bond was meant to be a protection against the danger of a terrible disease. This is a tremendous strength now. I do wonder whether it may become difficult for them to resolve this closeness as Kevin, Jr., needs to rebel in adolescence. As if sensing my thoughts, Kevin, Sr., said, "Kevin and I are getting into more battles lately. He won't do what I tell him without an argument."

"Good for Kevin. Maybe it's a sign of his daring to fight back again after all he's been through."

Valerie spoke up. "It's all I can do not to hover over him. Lauren came in the other day saying, 'Kevin just wiped out on his bike and he's knocked out.' I went to the door. There was Kevin flat on the street, face down. I held myself back and I just called out, 'Are you OK?' He mumbled, 'I'm OK,' and I let him get up by himself."

"By doing this you are saving him from . . ."

". . . a vulnerable child syndrome! I've read all your books. And I'm working on it, but it surely is hard."

Kevin began to look uncomfortable and went out to play.

"I know, but you are doing just the right thing," I said. "A boy who can handle a wipeout on his bike or a pounding from the neighbor kid without you having to stand up for him is going to feel secure inside himself. When parents feel the need to intervene for a child, it reinforces a sense of inadequacy in him. It makes him feel he's not equal to what other kids can handle. It can reinforce a sense of being different or damaged in the same way. Handling his own spills and fights is a great antidote to the feelings of being weak or bad or lazy or any of the things he might have felt as a very sick six-year-old."

In response to my reassurance, Valerie said, "But maybe we push him *too* much. We want so much for him – after all he's been through."

The McClay Family Revisited

"Of course, and a natural reaction would be to try to protect him from any further stress. But it wouldn't help him. Letting him deal with problems and see that he can do it is so much more strengthening for him."

Kevin, Sr., pursued this. "If he could only share his feelings more easily. Once he starts, it pours out. It's so much easier for the girls. Lauren will tell you everything she's feeling and be quite relaxed about it. He says, 'Same old junk' when we ask him what went on today."

I wondered whether "same old junk" didn't mean the same old fears of the future. It takes a child a long time to get over such a frightening episode. Everything else must seem trivial by comparison. But I agreed with their efforts to get him to communicate and to share his feelings with them, so I didn't make this interpretation of his struggle, for I felt it might have been too stressful for them. They are still caught up in their own struggle with his illness. Although he seems "miraculously" cured, a miracle carries with it a certain kind of disbelief, a sense of holding on for dear life. Underneath, Valerie and Kevin may still not dare to believe their son's recovery is real.

"Kevin is coming out of it," his father went on. "When the kid next door manipulates him, Kevin fights back now. He says, 'I'm not letting him take advantage of me.' He's coming out of his shell. Maybe that will help at school, too. He used to just tap on his desk when he was frustrated. The sisters complained about that. Now he says, 'You're wrong' to them, or, 'I don't understand that,' and they don't like that either, but I feel *he's* better off, whether they understand or not."

I agreed wholeheartedly.

"We don't go over and talk to them," said Valerie. "We don't want them to baby him, but are they going overboard? I learned when both my parents died when I was thirteen that you just have to get on with your life. You don't have choices. But you can learn something from such things. You can be a kind person. And always try to further yourself. That's the best you can do. I want Kevin to be like that. But are we too tough on him? When I tell him, 'Don't hit your sisters,' he looks at me as if I was too hard on him.

Once he said, 'You don't hug me like you do them.' That hit me below the belt. Am I doing the right thing?"

"You are trying to give him a feeling that he's really OK and can handle things without being babied. He needs that. But like any child, he needs the feeling that you are there when he needs you. Now may be the time, if he's in difficulty in school. Find out what the teachers are saying. Too much pressure on him isn't good either. It must take a child years and years to cope with all of the anger and emotions such a disease causes. I think you both have been terribly sensitive to this side of his struggle. I always wonder how tightly connected the physical and the psychological sides of recovery from a disease like this really are."

"We do, too," said Valerie. "When he was in the midst of the chemotherapy, I said to Kevin, 'We've got to help him with his feelings, too.' And we did. It helped us all to see a psychologist and to get involved in the support group we were in at the hospital." Valerie paused.

"When I married Kevin," she went on, "he was practically emotionless. He never expressed any of his feelings."

"Like Kevin, Jr.?"

"Well, maybe," she replied. "I never actually thought of it before. But Kevin, Sr., never showed joy or sadness. When young Kevin got sick, he began to open up. No, it started before that. Actually, it was Kevin being born that opened him up. That was the first miracle, having his own son. Kevin, Jr., and he have always been very, very close. They seem to know what each other is feeling, even without words."

"That's their way of communicating."

"True," said Valerie. "But I needed more from Kevin when young Kevin was sick. We all had to learn how to express ourselves. Kevin, Sr., has learned, too, or I wouldn't have made it. I'm Italian, and I can't hide emotions."

Kevin, Sr., nodded and agreed. "It helped all of us. We had to learn that."

As if this discussion triggered them to be more open with me, as well, they brought up a new issue: "We play musical beds in our family. Kevin likes to get in bed with his sisters, and he comes into our bed at night, too. He has a room by himself, but he never stays in it. Lauren stays in her bed. The baby stays in hers. But Kevin seems to be unable to sleep alone."

"I can't give advice without knowing more. Kevin may still be haunted by anxiety about separation, left over from the threat of his illness. Death to a young child means separation from all those he loves. That's the biggest fear – 'Where will I go? Will I be alone? Who will be there to take care of me?' Maybe he still hasn't worked out those fears, even though he is able to talk about going 'up there' to be with his grandparents."

"I never made that connection," said Valerie. "Do you think it would help him if we talked about that? It is pretty awkward to find him in our bed; one of us must move out. We never know where we'll end up sleeping. But in the face of what we've been through, I don't mind too much."

"Are you wondering whether this sleeping in others' beds is really good for Kevin?"

"Yes," said Valerie.

"I'm not sure it is, particularly as he enters adolescence. His closeness to you is great. But it may make it harder for him to find himself and to be able to separate as he should."

"Maybe we do need to think more about what this sleep business means to Kevin," said his father. "You know, after my mother and father died, we took their dog to live with us. We *all* loved him. Then the dog died. He was old, so we expected it. But Kevin fell apart. He began to pick on his sisters. This time, I knew what it was. I told him, 'Go up to your room and think about the dog and let yourself cry.' He came down, feeling a lot better. But he had to face death, again."

"How have the other children been handling his illness?" I asked.

"Stephanie was too young to really understand," said Valerie. "I don't think she's ever had to deal with it, and she's the most outgoing, determined child we've got. Lauren suffered the most. One night in the middle of his chemotherapy, Kevin woke up bleeding with mouth sores. She was in bed with him, and she woke up screaming. She had seen all the blood. She was hysterical. She cried out over and over, 'Did I make Kevin sick?' Ever since

The McClay Family

then, she's protected him. Now she's beginning to be less anxious, and she's getting more competitive with him. She's naturally shy and lets herself be taken advantage of. But now, with our urging, she's beginning to treat him as less fragile. She fights him. It took her a year and a half, but she's better." Valerie sighed. "It's hard to juggle more than one child through such a tough time."

Kevin, Sr., returned to something lingering on his mind: Was Kevin's inattention and daydreaming a form of hyperactivity? The nuns had forced them to think about such a label. They claimed that Kevin had such a short attention span and was so constantly active that he might have attention deficit disorder (known for short as ADD, or hyperactivity). Even though he was one of the top pupils in his class, they kept pushing. They even got so desperate that they suggested Ritalin (a drug especially designed to treat hyperactive children). The McClays felt that it wasn't right to treat him with a drug "unless he really needs it." Did I think he was hyperactive? Did he need Ritalin?

I had seen Kevin pay quiet attention earlier to all we were discussing and sit still listening for over an hour. He not only wasn't fidgety, but he wasn't even distracted. These are two characteristics of the syndrome of ADD. I told the McClays that I didn't feel he was truly hyperactive. I felt his illness had been such a blow to him that it still preoccupied him. The short attention span, the daydreaming that they saw in school, came out when he was under pressure, and seemed quite appropriate. These symptoms represented an underlying turmoil; when he was in balance, he could do all that they wanted of him. But when he felt he was failing, or not pleasing the teachers, he became distractible and hard to reach.

"I wonder if I put him under more pressure by saying, 'You can't play hockey if you don't succeed in conquering your problems at school.' Is that more pressure?"

"I would think so. Kevin might well be able to manage all of this at once. He's such a remarkable boy. But he's only nine years old. The nuns don't recognize this need for a safety valve. They want an attentive, conforming child and as long as Kevin is that, they are satisfied. But he needs outlets, too. I, too, would hate to see you put him on medication. For him, especially, drugs must

The McClay Family Revisited

have a deeper meaning. They probably mean all of the things that his illness meant — being sad, weird, damaged. I would rather see him under less pressure, allowed to take his time in school."

"Do you think we should go back to the counselor we saw with him before?" asked Valerie. "She helped us so much."

"That might be a good step. You deserve to have someone else help. If she understands Kevin and he likes her, I'd think it would give him a chance to develop some new ways of working out any unresolved issues around his illness, and she might well help all of you develop techniques for handling any stress which comes in the future."

The fact that the McClays' attempt to look at the bright side of such a monumental threat as their son's illness did not entirely do away with all the stress is not surprising. The way denial helped them survive the period of diagnosis and treatment is amazing enough. Now they were in enough balance to face the remaining pain, the uncertainty, the incomprehensible aspects of their experience. Maybe this will reassure Kevin and help him find his way. Given time, Kevin is likely to be a leader and achieve all he wants in school. This will please him and his parents, and they surely deserve some victories.

As I left, I felt a sense of awe and of gratitude to this remarkable family who had let me come so close. They had allowed me into the depths of their ordeal. Now I could really appreciate their "miracle," as I watched that glowing nine-year-old. As I left, he raced down the little dead-end street with his stuntboard, sailing high into the air, landing on the ground with a thud, still upright and still able to show me how fearless he was after all he'd been through. I joined them all in believing that God was certainly on Kevin's side!

The McClay Family

The O'Connell-Beder Family

CHAPTER V

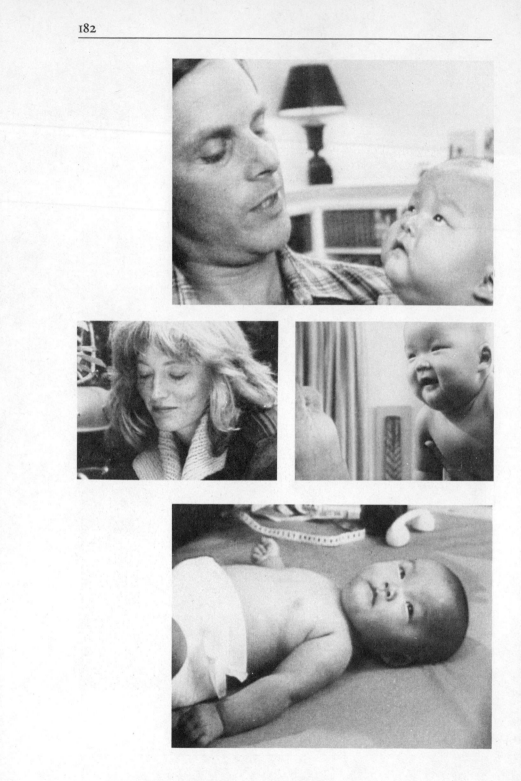

The O'Connell-Beder Family

Family History

૨૾

Eileen O'Connell and Barry Beder are the parents of Jenny, a four-month-old Korean baby whom they adopted one month ago. Eileen is a psychiatric nurse, who has been in private practice for ten years. She cut the practice down to part time in order to be free to accept any adoption that came along. Eileen is tall and blond, and she has a confident air about her. Barry Beder, dark, clean-cut, is a championship tennis player and the picture of a successful young executive. He runs a consulting business in stress reduction and corporate health programs. Using new concepts based upon hypnosis and his background in social work, he conducts seminars for businesses all over the country on how to handle stress, alcoholism, and smoking. His success has been rapid and somewhat overwhelming to him. He now has an office staff of several people, but has to do most of the consulting himself. So far, he has traveled a great deal, but he has been trying to cut down recently so that he can be more available to his wife and to the new baby.

Eileen and Barry first met as they jointly led a group for adolescents in a psychiatric hospital. Like many couples today, they had waited until their careers were established and they were stable as a couple to start a family. They expected that Eileen would get pregnant right away. When she didn't, they were shocked.

Eight years of harrowing examinations and treatment for their infertility followed. The experience was devastating to them, as individuals and as a married couple, bringing up feelings of inadequacy, grief, helplessness, and anger. These feelings were irrational and difficult to control. The insecurities which most of us experience as we grow up were revived by this deep wound to their self-esteem. Eileen and Barry had become accustomed to success. Because their marriage and careers were thriving, they had every reason to feel sure of success in starting a family. Though they both enjoyed their work, they also looked upon it as an investment for their future family. Everything about them was ready and waiting. But no baby came.

The O'Connell-Beder Family

Infertility

ҽ♠

OFFICE VISIT

During Eileen and Barry's first visit to my office, we addressed their problems with infertility. I needed to understand what they'd been through, so that I could get to know them and to help them get a good start with Jenny. Eileen seemed hungry to discuss their experience, and Barry seemed eager to participate as well. Their need for support was both appealing and touching.

EILEEN   It's a long story. I'd spent all of my adult life trying not to get pregnant, and so when I – we – decided to have a baby, I virtually was ready to start sending out the birth announcements – you know, nine months from the time that we start trying, of course, our child will be born.

BARRY   Actually, the first time we went to the gynecologist, we went together, and the gynecologist said that Eileen was ovulating just then, so we ran home. I called my office and said, "I'm going home to make a baby, folks."

EILEEN   The only question was whether it was going to be a boy or a girl.

BARRY   Right. It was to be as easy as that.

EILEEN   And then, nothing.

Eileen and Barry kept trying. Months became years. They searched for help. What they found was more frustration.

BARRY · They could find nothing wrong. They diagnosed us as "normal infertile," meaning the doctors just didn't know. They kept putting us off, saying, "Well, maybe this and maybe that," then they came up with another test. Finally, they did find something, about four years into it.

DR. BRAZELTON · Four years that you were having tests!

BARRY · On and off.

EILEEN · They found an infection in both of us, and they said, "That's it. Take these pills for twelve days. They'll make you nauseous, but put up with it and then you'll get pregnant."

BARRY · They did make us nauseous. They got that right. But that's about it. No pregnancy. By then, it seemed like all our friends were having babies or had young children, and it was hard being around them.

DR. BRAZELTON · Every time you'd look at a baby, you'd feel . . .

BARRY · Right. A lot of times in a movie, or a commercial on television, there'd be a baby, and we'd kind of look at each other, and it would make us sad.

EILEEN · Barry, you would usually say, "It'll happen." And I'd cry. I'd be sitting in the movies and there'd be a mother-baby scene, and I would start to cry. *I hear this same story so many times.*

DR. BRAZELTON · Did each of you feel inadequate?

The O'Connell-Beder Family

BARRY

When I was with men, sometimes they would crack macho jokes. They'd say, "Don't you know how to do it?" That kind of thing. "Want me to show you how to do it?"

DR. BRAZELTON   Men would say that to you?

BARRY

Jokingly, you know. They'd say, "Hey, you'd better get working on it," or, "What's the matter?"

DR. BRAZELTON   You're a championship tennis player, aren't you? Did it begin to interfere with your sports?

BARRY

No. I found a way of working out some of those feelings and anger on the tennis court.

DR. BRAZELTON   Yet it's bound to hit your feelings about yourself as a male and, Eileen, it must hit your feelings about your femininity.

EILEEN

Yes, I began to feel like I wasn't a real woman. Something very deep-seated was wrong with me. I felt I was not attractive, not desirable. Sometimes I'd think that there was something about me that . . .

DR. BRAZELTON   . . . was a sham?

EILEEN

Yes. People all around were producing these children, and I was trying so hard, but nothing was happening. Things built up over a period of time and came to a crisis when we no longer knew if we wanted to be married to each other. We had reached the point where we were even questioning that. I began to imagine that when he was forty-five years old or so, he would fall in love with a nineteen-year-old and have children with her, and then it all would be fine for him. He didn't have to feel the biological pressure. Part of me began to question whether he would be married to me for the long haul.

BARRY Her fantasies were right, in a sense. Not that I had any intention of leaving her, but it would have been a lot easier at that point to leave her than to stay. It was a real test of our marriage.

EILEEN I think that threat to our marriage made me decide to stop trying to get pregnant. I tended to be the one who felt the pressure most acutely. I just couldn't keep on trying. After sixty-some cycles, I said, "That's *all*! I can't do this anymore. I have to stop, because this is making me crazy." Once we made the decision to adopt, it was liberating. I felt like we took a very long, hard journey together and somehow made it through – came out the other end. And this is what makes it feel so special about having Jenny.

BARRY It's like a party all the time now.

DR. BRAZELTON I know. That miracle, that baby. She's so great, isn't she?

THE ISSUES

More and more couples are waiting to start their families until they are in their early or mid-thirties. Using birth control techniques to assure them of a choice about the timing of the first baby, they may dream and plan for several years before they start to try.

The O'Connell-Beder Family

Having been successful in other areas, they are programmed for success in this one, too. When it works as planned, they are unlikely to be either surprised or grateful. Pregnancy fits their expectation that "When we are ready, it will happen."

When these midcareer, midthirties couples become parents, they can offer their baby an established, secure environment. They can also offer the baby a model of inner security which they have built up in these years of success. They are likely to become dedicated parents. At the same time, the vicissitudes of relating to a baby and of accepting a deepened sense of responsibility often throw them for a while. Couples at this age are likely to be rather set in their ways, and yet each new stage in the baby's development demands reorganization on their part. Therefore they are likely to be anxious along the way as parents. For a pediatrician, they are demanding as patients, because they care so much and want to do everything well. They seek more advice than younger people do. They work hard to understand the psychology of parenting and of child rearing – often when there aren't easy explanations. The unknowns of parenting tend to upset them. They tend to hover over the baby. Parenting demands both learning by mistakes and letting a child do the same; young professionals who have planned and controlled their lives up to this point must learn a new approach as parents. All this is not easy, but because these couples are so eager to be parents, their powerful motivation helps them learn fast. Their eagerness, anxiety, and turmoil loosens up their set ways.

Sometimes, however, becoming a parent in the first place is hard. The long torment of infertility testing and attempted treatments undermines the expectation of success in couples like Barry and Eileen. Taking a daily temperature to predict ovulation, holding off on sexual activity until the precise moment, wondering whether potency will be maintained – all this routine clouds the sexual act between two caring people. Then, waiting each month for the miracle, adding up disappointments with each new menstrual period, builds anxiety and tension. The male must be tested, examined, sperm gathered by a degrading masturbation at the clinic. When sperm are counted and checked for motility, it may seem as if masculinity is being measured. The man must wonder,

"Am I all right?" After months of failure, the answer seems clear: of course, he's not all right, unless . . . it's his wife's fault. The unconscious hope that it's she and not he who is infertile makes him feel guilty toward his wife. These feelings alternate with feelings of inadequacy. Most men yearn to go outside the marriage to *prove* it's not their fault. The danger to the marriage of an extramarital affair becomes a constant fantasy, even if it is not acted upon.

A woman's infertility workup is likely to be even more intrusive, demeaning, and sometimes painful. Every aspect of her genital tract, of her ovaries and their function is studied in repetitious detail. Can she even make eggs? Are they defective? Does she have irregular menses? Is she unable to nurture a fertilized egg and to hold on to it? Interviews involve intimate questions: "Do you like sex? Do you like it with your husband? Have you ever had affairs before and gotten infections that could have ruined your reproductive tract? Could this all be psychosomatic? If you'd relax and weren't so tense, maybe you'd have a baby." All of these raise both spoken and unspoken anxieties. They are always present in an infertile woman's mind. When a doctor in the clinic looks at her, she sees these questions in the doctor's eyes. When a new nurse examines her, or tests her, she knows that these questions are in the nurse's mind. After all, they are in hers.

When infertile couples must face their families, old struggles can be revived. For instance, "Why did you marry a Jewish boy? Why wasn't Catholic good enough? Maybe God is willing this." Or: "A Jewish girl would have given you all the babies you want. It's not right to marry outside the faith. It breaks down the purity of our family heritage." "We always worried about your marriage. Maybe if this one doesn't work, you can give it up and marry a good [Catholic, Jewish, Protestant, Chinese, etc.] girl. We'd understand and be so happy." Even if families don't express such thoughts, infertile couples are likely to feel they are there.

As more and more contemporaries produce babies, these become a constant reminder of failure. Infertile couples find it excruciating to be around happy, gushing parents with a new baby.

For an adult to accept a failure as important as the inability to reproduce, grieving must take place. Not only is there grief for the loss of the imagined baby and for the chance to reproduce

The O'Connell-Beder Family

oneself, but there is also pain in the injury to self-image. Throughout our lives, we struggle to feel competent. Each threat to our feelings of competence and self-esteem generates an alarm reaction. This, in turn, produces extra energy to confront the threat and reactivates similar previous experiences. We regress and reorganize to handle the challenge. When we succeed, we are strengthened, and another positive learning experience is added to our resources. If success is impossible, as in infertility, we grieve for our failure.

Depression and a sense of inadequacy accompany grief. Anger often follows: "Why me?" The defenses, already mentioned, that we all use in the face of loss are set up: (1) denial – "It's not true, or certainly not my fault"; (2) projection – "It's him [or her], not me"; and (3) detachment – because it's so painful to care. These defenses are an inevitable part of the experience of infertility and must be recognized so that they don't become a way of life. If they are openly discussed and seen as inevitable but temporary feelings, they are less apt to endanger a marriage and other relationships.

After a while, one or the other or both members of an infertile couple will move on from grief to think of adoption, or of ways to build a nurturing, productive, fruitful life without children. Whatever solution a couple chooses, however, it is still important to their own relationship with each other and to any child they might adopt to realize that these feelings will still be there. Each new stress and failure will revive the pangs, each new success and challenge well met will mitigate them. The times when they come up again are likely to be at each of the normal stress points encountered as a child grows up. Anything that gives parents a sense of failure, which all parents experience, will awaken greater doubt in adoptive parents. If they can understand and accept such feelings as a normal, expectable reaction, they won't need to be at their mercy as they meet the universal vicissitudes of parenting. When an adoptive child gets stuck in a behavior pattern – for instance, in such normal ones as negativism at two, lying at four, stealing at five, or adolescent turmoil – adoptive parents can worry excessively. They can blame the child for "bad genes," or themselves for not caring enough. Such worries can be destructive, compounding every normal hurdle for an adoptive family. Adoptive parents who are prepared, by self-understanding and by knowledge of the inevitable stages and pitfalls in child development, can stop asking themselves, "Would I have been a better parent to the baby I might have had if only . . . ?"

COMMON CONCERNS

One of the most helpful ways for couples to learn to deal with infertility is to join a support group with other couples who are facing the same difficulty. In such groups, couples learn that all of their reactions are universal and normal. No expert can advise ways of coping as well as other couples who are up against the same diagnosis. Thus, rather than attempting to answer common questions myself, I have selected and transcribed taped excerpts from the sessions of an actual infertility support group which I attended. Names and a few details are disguised for confidentiality.

DR. BRAZELTON   How many women felt that infertility was their problem and not their husbands'?

JANE   I did, because I was the one going through all the tests, and although my husband was very supportive, they really didn't ask him to do much, other than come in and help me out, or come in and we'll do a husband insemination. It was always me that had to have everything done. I felt angry and hopelessly inadequate at times. Every month was a horror of waiting. I said, "Maybe this month," but it never was.

NED   With us, it was the opposite. The problem seemed to be with me, at first. And I think Sally was feeling guilty, because I had to go through a lot. I had to go in for surgery twice, and she kept saying, "Why aren't they doing tests on me?" Since they felt that my sperm

The O'Connell-Beder Family

count was low, there was no need to start any workups on her.

SALLY   Our first doctor felt there was no reason to put me through any testing. Since his sperm count was so low, the chances of my getting pregnant were hopeless. But I had always seen Ned as a person who could do anything. If he decided that he wanted to do something, he was always the type of person who would put his mind to it and do it. But here was this one thing that was so important to both of us that he couldn't do. It made me look at him in a very different, more human kind of way. It was terrible for him, really, and I hated myself for feeling pity.

EMILY   My problem was picked up when I was still in nursing school, and we married knowing that we might not be able to have children. That wasn't so much of an issue at the time, when we were so young. We thought about it, but until we actually tried and found out that we were having difficulty, it didn't hit home. When we started the testing, there were minor problems with my husband's sperm counts. They were not serious, but still he was put through a lot of tests. I felt guilty because my endometriosis is the overriding factor, and here they were putting him through all this. I've gone through medical treatment. I've gone through surgery and have more coming up. My husband takes it well, but I have the fear that maybe he would rather go away and marry someone else.

SALLY   What this issue does for a couple's sexual relationship is something I'm sure all of us have

Infertility

had to deal with. I know that, for us, to have sex means to try to have a baby. If we aren't going to have a baby, then why have sex? And to get that desire back again, to have a sexual relationship separate from trying to make a baby, I think is something that's still very difficult.

NED I feel like the fellow on the Dunkin' Donuts commercial – time to make the baby, time to make the baby. Each time, a man has to perform. Let's face it, it can be hard. This goal of a baby is like a butterfly – the more you chase it, the more elusive it becomes. Sometimes I think that if we could just sit and be quiet, the butterfly would come to us. I think of pregnancy like that.

DR. BRAZELTON Magical.

NED Yes, I think so. I really, truly believe that.

JANE In some ways, we were more fortunate. After we went through extensive testing, I found out that I had total ovarian failure. So once I knew that there was no way I could have children, it was easier for us to make the decision – now, either we decide to adopt or we don't have any children.

MARY That was our initial diagnosis, too. I felt that if we weren't going to have any children, I didn't want to be married.

DR. BRAZELTON Did you really feel like splitting at that point?

MARY I did. But my husband wouldn't let me and then we had a child. That's why it's so impor-

The O'Connell-Beder Family

tant to keep trying, going to doctors, though you want to give up.

JOHN   I think it's important to draw a line, though, because otherwise, there is no end. You keep trying and trying and going through more surgery. The pain of all that and the emotional agony that you go through and the worry . . . you have to draw the line. But, then again, from Emily's point of view, she's willing to go through as much pain and agony as she has to to make it happen. It's so important to her. It's important to me, too, but not to the point of risking my wife's life. Sometimes I get to the point where I'm a little worried about that.

EMILY   I don't see it that way. I feel I'll make it through and be OK. I just feel driven. People have asked me about this drive and, as I've spoken with other infertile couples, it is an amazing drive to me. I wonder what possesses us to continue this pursuit, but I do find that people are very strong.

GEORGE   We adopted a son. To me, the bottom line is to have a child and to be a parent.

NED   I'm not sure that I'm at that point yet, although I can still remember a line from Shakespeare, "Die single and thine image dies with thee." I don't think that's being egotistical, but it's more part of the male psyche than the female – just wanting to carry on your name and producing something that you could leave behind. Something tangible. And I'm not talking about constructing a building or something like that, but something that's going to *live* on far after you're gone – your own child.

Infertility

ALICE   When we adopted, I felt a loss because I hadn't been pregnant. I didn't bring this child into the world.

MICHAEL   For us, making the decision to adopt was drawing the line. We said to ourselves, "Well, we're almost giving up on having our own baby anytime in the near future so, instead, we're going to start this process to get a baby by adoption." That was a very difficult decision to make. We put it off for a couple of years.

JANE   I think I lost my dream baby a while ago, so I don't compare our adopted baby. I don't know why. I've just accepted him as a little person on his own, and he's wonderful.

The O'Connell-Beder Family

Adoption

OFFICE VISIT

Jenny Beder, lying in Eileen's lap, is a beautiful, doll-like Korean baby. But she isn't like Eileen and Barry, and they are having a hard time believing she could be theirs.

EILEEN She was three months when we got her, and we haven't a clue what it was like for her until then. The first time she cried after she came, I did not know what she wanted. I felt so bad, because I thought she was asking for something that had been part of her routine, and I didn't know what her routine had been. She'd already lived a whole life before I got her.

DR. BRAZELTON You felt like – "If I'd just been there all that time."

EILEEN That's right.

Even after a month, they still felt Jenny was a stranger and wondered whether she was really all right.

EILEEN When she slept, she slept with her legs pulled up and her arms pulled in, and when I would go in and check her, three hours would pass and she would be in the same position. She wouldn't have turned her head.

DR. BRAZELTON Sort of a fetal position.

BARRY	In fact, the first week – remember? The first week, she almost didn't cry. The first time she cried, she gave, like, a whimper.
EILEEN	She cried politely.
DR. BRAZELTON	As if she didn't expect any response.
EILEEN	Maybe.

All three of us wondered what that environment was before she came – whether it was really nurturing. In response to these worries – so common in adoptions – I decided to perform a few developmental tests. I held her extended arms, pulling her up to sit. Instead, she came right up to a standing position, grinning and looking around.

EILEEN	From the day she arrived, she's wanted to stand.
BARRY	Don't you love the way she stands? She holds her arms out straight, perfectly straight, like she's flying.
DR. BRAZELTON	Now let's see you crawl.

For most babies, four months is a transition stage – from automatic reflexes to more voluntary actions. Jenny is becoming more actively motivated to get where she's going. No longer is her crawling automatic; she works toward a goal. By now, a lot of the newborn reflexes, like the walking and crawling reflex, have dropped out. Such reflexes are automatic, originating in a lower part of the brain. By four months, they are being replaced by deliberate motions: crawling, reaching, pushing. The behavior of a four-month-old baby is a mixture of automatic and deliberate actions.

The O'Connell-Beder Family

DR. BRAZELTON See how I can mobilize her reach by just touching her hand. When I do that, it stimulates her to reach for the toy I'm holding.

BARRY I want to make sure we're not missing something important.

DR. BRAZELTON Like what?

BARRY Something we don't know about that happens between a biological parent and child. How can I tell?

His question told me something. I thought I knew what might be behind it. A sensitive child like Jenny, in her new environment, might be shutting down on them when they became too eager. I overstimulated her on purpose. Jenny then showed us how she dealt with overload. She shut her eyes, she averted her head. She became limp. I could get no more responses from her.

DR. BRAZELTON She's had all she wants from me. Does she tune you out like that?

EILEEN Yes. There was a period when she would look me right in the eye and just give a blank expression, and then she would turn away and go back to cooing, or whatever it was. It used to break my heart. I thought, "Oh, my God. She doesn't like me!"

DR. BRAZELTON With that kind of look, a baby can make you feel inadequate. *Eileen's real worry.*

EILEEN The feeling that I got was that she wanted to be back with her biological mother. She had figured out that I was now going to take care of her, and I thought she was letting me know that I wasn't so hot. *Eileen and Barry were wondering if their adopted daughter would ever really be theirs.*

DR. BRAZELTON   So you felt really rejected. Not just inadequate, but *rejected. They both looked at me for reassurance, the kind that only Jenny could give.* Let's try an experiment. You both get out of the way now. All right. Now, first I want Mommy to come in and start talking to her.

EILEEN   *Softly coos.* "Jenny."

DR. BRAZELTON   She's still looking off into the distance, but watch her hands and arms. See how the way they move has become smoother. Look at her and her hands going like this as she hears your voice. Now see how she comes back to look at your face, softens and takes it in, and then goes back to looking off into the distance again.

EILEEN   When she sees me, she almost looks delighted.

DR. BRAZELTON   Say something without coming closer, Barry.

BARRY   *Softly.* "Hello, hello."

DR. BRAZELTON   Watch Jenny's shoulders go up, she gets sort of giddy when she hears him; there's a whole different language between the two of them.

Jenny arched her shoulders, her eyebrows, as if she knew Barry's voice and anticipated his coming to play with her.

DR. BRAZELTON   For Jenny, this is a very overwhelming new world and very scary. When she arrived, you wanted to get to her so quickly that you may have pushed too hard and made her pull back.

The O'Connell-Beder Family

You know, this adjustment is what attachment is all about. You're so sensitive to her, and she obviously is getting so much from you and taking it in, in her own way. She's got a language now all her own, and that language is the language of attachment. Look at her, holding her mother's finger and playing with it. That isn't a baby who's being neglected. If she ever was, she's certainly making up for it. All these signs of attachment that she shows become so important, don't they, because they let you know . . .

EILEEN   . . . that it's going OK for her. That means it's going to go great from our end!

THE ISSUES

Adoption is a lifelong job – infinitely rewarding but tough at times. Not only is the decision to adopt a major one, but the adjustment to the role can be difficult. Adjusting to a new baby is hard for any parent, but for adoptive parents there is an extra level of adjustment because they usually have yearned to be parents for so long. The more parents care about being the best possible parents for their baby, the more they have to worry about.

In a pregnancy, the fetus's development helps begin the adjustment. As the expectant parents prepare themselves with their wishes, their dreams, their anxieties, the fetus begins to move. The movement and the baby's style *in utero* help the parents experience the reality of the coming baby. Before an adoption, parents also dream and form wishes and fears about what the baby will be like. They are afraid it won't be normal, won't be like them. Today, with our rapidly increasing knowledge of the effects of intrauterine experiences – such as malnutrition, drugs, smoking, caffeine, infections – adoptive parents are bound to worry about what their baby has been exposed to before they are able to take over. How was my baby nurtured for the first nine months? If the child is adopted from another country, the unknown looms even larger. The influence of genetic factors, versus the environmental ones which the parents can begin to control, is an accentuated question in adoptions. What kind of woman would ever give up her baby? What was the father like? Is there inherited disease in the family? Were the parents intelligent? Regardless of what information is available from an agency or privately, worries about the genetics and the early intrauterine environment will be strong.

For adoptive parents, all of this questioning about origin can serve to raise the kind of anxiety and self-questioning which occurs during a normal pregnancy. If parents can utilize this anxious energy to help them try to understand and relate to the new adoptive baby as an individual, it can strengthen the bonding process. Ideally, parents will have the opportunity to observe the baby's reactions and behavior with a knowledgeable professional who can identify and interpret the baby's temperament, her reactions to stimuli, her individual use of sleep and alert states to control her environment. Sharing these observations gives the doctor or nurse a chance to lead the new parents toward an understanding of the baby as a person. I felt that I could help Eileen and Barry most if I played with Jenny. I wanted them to *see* her individuality, not merely hear about it from me. I knew that if they could understand her style and her temperament, it would give them a sense of competence in dealing with her. If her behavior remained strange or opaque, this could become a barrier as they tried to reach out and nurture her. Any questions they brought to me were not only specific questions to be answered but also reflected their deep-seated anxiety about her past.

During this time, adoptive parents are also gradually giving up the fantasied baby that they might have had together. Each of them has dreamed of a baby that looks like one or the other of them. Such dreams will never entirely vanish. But they must give up, as much as possible, this imaginary baby, in order to be available to their real baby. Otherwise, they will constantly compare the adopted baby to the one that might have been. For instance, whenever Jenny does something that reminds Barry of Eileen, he may catch himself before he blurts out, "She's just like you!" Or if

Jenny begins to imitate her father's playful giggles, Eileen may pause before she says, "She's learning to imitate your giggle!" The baby's very real identification with adoptive parents will make them ask, "Can she ever really be like him – or me? How much of her can we really claim?" These instinctive attributions, which are part of learning about one's baby's traits, are an easy part of a natural parent's experience, but must constantly be questioned and weighed by adoptive parents. If they can gradually forget the comparisons and enjoy the way the baby picks up all their ways, the rewards of parenthood can grow without regrets.

COMMON QUESTIONS

QUESTION What is the best time to start talking to a child about adoption?

DR. BRAZELTON One should always talk about it. There is never a best time. By three or four years, a child will have specific questions, and you should be prepared to answer them. "Where do I come from? Why didn't my parents want me? Were they bad? Will I ever get to meet my parents? Are you my real mother and father?" Such questions are inevitable, so it is wise to prepare for them. If you don't know much about the real parents, tell the child what you do know. Meet every question as honestly and directly as you can. The questions of an adopted child must be treated with respect. If asked why a mother might give up her child, you can feel secure in saying "to give you a better future than she could provide," or, if such was the case, that "she was unmarried and couldn't provide the family that she wanted for you."

Adoption

QUESTION   What if my child asks whether her birth mother still loves her?

DR. BRAZELTON   You might answer, "How could anyone not love you? She would if she knew you. I wanted you because I could see how wonderful you were. I wanted to be your family, and I am. I'm part of your family, and you're part of mine. I'll never leave you nor you me. If you ever want to find your birth mother, I'll help you. But you'll still be part of my family." A child needs to know that she is, and deserves to be, treasured, since the threat of desertion always looms for adopted children. The other thing a child needs to know is that she is part of a real family and will always be. An adopted child often reasons that if one mother can send her away, the adoptive parent might also – particularly if she's bad. Too many adoptive children suppress any negative feelings or negative behaviors for fear of being rejected again.

QUESTION   My son was adopted through an agency in Bogota, Colombia, and they gave no case history. Their records just say "abandoned" on them. My son will want to know why he was "abandoned." I've gotten various opinions – make up a story, tell him the truth: that we really don't know. What do you suggest?

DR. BRAZELTON   The word "abandoned" does have frightening implications. I would recommend saying that you think his mother probably would never have "let him go" if she hadn't been so poor, and so worried that she couldn't feed him or take care of him well. She must have loved him a great deal and wanted him to have a better life. Since you know where he came from, you can also learn about his former culture and stress its strengths to him. When he's older, he can learn more on his own. A child with a sure sense of his own cultural heritage will be proud of it.

QUESTION We learned quite suddenly that our baby daughter was ready for us about two weeks before she came. So we rushed out to buy everything – clothes, a crib, and so on. But at the time, I got a strong sad feeling. It was almost like an anxiety attack. I really couldn't explain it, and I wondered why I felt that way before she came, when I should have been so excited.

DR. BRAZELTON The anxiety and depression that come with such a major step as an adoption is the other side of the coin. Elation often dominates, but anxiety is normal, as well. During this time, you are still working to give up the fantasy of a natural child. So anxiety and even depression are part of the adjustment. If one can acknowledge these feelings, as you are doing, the adjustment will be more complete. This ambivalence is part of an "alarm" reaction, releasing adrenaline and causing other bodily reactions to help meet the major adjustment. If an adoptive parent is all optimism, I worry about her. It means that she is allowing herself to feel only one side of the adjustment. Depression and negative feelings are likely to follow later.

QUESTION We adopted our little boy when he was already two years old. He's been with us two weeks now and still seems awfully quiet and sad. How can we help him feel at home?

Adoption

DR. BRAZELTON   A two-year-old is likely to become negative when he gets sure enough of himself, so negativism and temper tantrums will be a good sign of his recovery. At first, he's bound to be withdrawn and depressed. If he's had a good, nurturant foster placement, he'll mourn about the readjustment and is likely to mourn for at least a month or so, before he will allow you to get close to him. His mourning will probably not take the form of open weeping or resistance; it will be a more passive withdrawal. You should feel relieved when he lets you see other sides of him. If he's had a bad placement previously, he will be disorganized and difficult to engage or to relate to. He may be unruly or unreachable at first. He may resist being held or cuddled, because he once lost all that and it's too painful. You must be patient and persistent, but sensitive to how afraid he may be to trust the kind of loving you want to give him. The more he longs for it, the more he may need to resist it. Your wooing may take a long time. I would predict a six-month period before he and you feel secure with each other. Don't take it personally.

QUESTION   We have a three-year-old daughter of our own and have just adopted a five-year-old boy. She seems quite hostile to him.

DR. BRAZELTON   Expect her to resent it, and don't get too upset by her resentment. Try to enlist her in helping the newcomer adjust. When she finally learns to share you and her house and her toys with her adopted brother, she will have learned an important lesson for her future. But she needn't like it. Help her understand her negative feelings, and let her see that you can take

The O'Connell-Beder Family

them. But never let her feel that she can actually get rid of her brother just because she wishes to. That would frighten her, indeed. As you enlist her help, give her as much understanding of your son's situation as you can. Let her see when she is making it with her new brother, and encourage her to believe they will have a good time in the long run. Leave them to work out their rivalry on their own. They'll get to be better friends, and more quickly, if you stay out of their relationship. As he begins to become more secure, he'll start acting out. Your reaction will probably be: "This is what he learned from his previous home. I don't want her exposed to it." It won't hurt her. She may even imitate him, but she won't assume his behavior permanently. As she mimics him, she will be getting closer to him, learning more about him. As he expresses his negative feelings, he will become more secure. So your job is to let all this happen.

QUESTION   We have an adopted daughter and a son who was born to us earlier. I've experienced feelings with him that I haven't felt with her. Will that continue?

DR. BRAZELTON   The job of sorting out your feelings about your own child and an adopted one may become increasingly demanding. Your son may say, "You don't love me. You had to go get her." Or she will say, "You love him more than me, because I'm adopted." Even when their rivalry is unspoken, you will feel the tug of trying to equalize your responses and your feelings. You are likely to lean over backward trying to treat them equally. You can't. You are bound to feel differently about two children. It is a myth or wishful thinking to imagine that you can feel exactly the same way about each. By trying to, you'll inhibit your relations with them. Each of them means something different to you, and needs a different side of you. Acknowledge your different feelings. Level with both children about what you respect and care about in each one, and point out that each one needs a different set of limits and concerns from you. They will have to learn to live with different treatment because they're very different people – not because one is yours and one isn't. If each one feels special and has time alone with your full attention, all this will balance out.

QUESTION   How can I deal with the time when my daughter wants to see her biological parents?

DR. BRAZELTON   You'll feel deserted and jealous. You'll feel that you haven't made her love you enough or she wouldn't need the other parents. These possessive feelings are entirely natural. To feel competitive and threatened by the natural parents is unavoidable. But you can also see her side of it. She wants to know as much as she can about herself, which includes knowing about them. I'd join her in her search and in her attempt to find them. In that way, you can support her through whatever she must find. You'll be there as her rock of Gibraltar, and she'll know it. Don't worry. She will know and value her "real" family more than ever. This is a test of herself and of her roots – one that each of us needs to make in order to feel like a whole person.

The O'Connell-Beder Family

What Will My Child Be Like?

≥♦

OFFICE VISIT

On their next visit to my office with Jenny, Barry and Eileen asked
me if I could tell what she would be like as she grew up, in build
and in personality. This kind of curiosity is a part of their caring.
It is evidence of their attachment to Jenny.

EILEEN   We are a little concerned about her rapid gain
                in weight – not so much for now, but what it
                might mean in terms of –

BARRY   – later on. Will she be fat later?

DR. BRAZELTON   There is some research showing that the num-
                ber of fat cells you lay down at this age will
                predict the number you'll have later on. But
                who knows how many you have or need?

EILEEN   She's been standing when we hold her hands
                since she was three months. Does this mean
                she'll walk early?

DR. BRAZELTON   I really don't know. Not necessarily.

Every parent wants a crystal ball, especially when a child is of
a different race. Eileen and Barry are bound to read this into almost
every bit of behavior.

BARRY   We have no idea where she came from. We
                don't know her family history. Genetically, we
                don't know what she was born with.

EILEEN   What can you tell about her personality?

DR. BRAZELTON   I don't think we really know what her personality is going to be like yet, because she's just blossoming now from her newborn experiences.

BARRY   Can we tell anything? For instance, I've noticed that she loves to look around – her visual sense is so strong. Does that tell us something about her as an adult?

DR. BRAZELTON   Well, it may. Certainly, Asian babies – I've been observing and playing with newborns in Japan and China – have twice as long an attention span and twice as much investment in visual and auditory stimuli as Caucasian newborns. They also show much quieter motor behavior, like hers, much gentler, sort of ballet-like movements, as newborns. So maybe there's a slight genetic factor here.

EILEEN   A predisposition.

DR. BRAZELTON   Right. And in that sense, it may predict to some extent what kind of person she's going to be. What I keep seeing is how lovely and quiet her states of consciousness are. You know, she stays alert for such a long time. There's one thing I'd like to try out with her . . . just watch her eyes. *I clap my hands a number of times.* Did you see that? Did you watch her eyes? Every single time, as I clap, she's blinked. She is extremely sensitive, and she hasn't got a very good way to shut out loud stimuli yet. She's still at the mercy of them. You'll have to respect that and try to give her a fairly quiet environment for sleep and play periods. After I quit clapping, look what happened. She started fussing. But you rushed right to her, so we never saw what she was like when she was fussing. I don't think I can stop you, though.

EILEEN   Mother instinct. *She smiles.*

BARRY   She got there first. I was going to grab Jenny, too.

Barry and Eileen were so sensitive, so responsive, and so hungry for information.

EILEEN   It is still hard for me not to respond when she fusses.

DR. BRAZELTON   That's because you are still learning about one another. Every time she gives you a cue, you're dying to get it, dying to understand it.

EILEEN   The first few days, it was hard not to pick her up. I couldn't wait for her to wake up so I could grab her.

BARRY   I keep trying out new things to see what she'll do. We've invented a game where we pick her up and as we pick her up, she starts to laugh, and then she'll start saying, "Ai – ai – ." And then she'll start crying when it gets too much.

EILEEN   That little giggle is new, too – this week.

DR. BRAZELTON   She's adding on new things every day, isn't she?

EILEEN   It's really exciting.

BARRY   Sometimes she'll be sitting in a group of people, five or six people all sitting around, and

What Will My Child Be Like?

she'll look from one person to the next to the next, always looking and smiling at people. Does that mean she's going to be social? Does that say something about her?

DR. BRAZELTON   I'll say yes to that one.

BARRY   Oh?

DR. BRAZELTON   Partly because of you. The best predictor I've got is you.

EILEEN   A lot of babies seem to have to be kept away from people. She's so comfortable with everyone. I guess we're wondering whether that trait is likely to stay. *There is something behind those words.*

DR. BRAZELTON   I'm not quite sure what you are asking. Will she stay sociable? Is that what you mean?

EILEEN   Well, when I walk down the street with her, we don't get half a block without being stopped. We look so different. I feel like it's always going to be an issue and wonder how she'll react.

DR. BRAZELTON   I thought that was it.

EILEEN   I want her to feel comfortable if she's questioned, because I think she will be, the way I am now. People ask, and I try to be comfortable saying, "Yes, she's from Korea."

DR. BRAZELTON   They look at her and look at you and then look around for the Asian father.

The O'Connell-Beder Family

EILEEN   Right. And sort of wait for the explanation, and I would like her to have the social skills to –

DR. BRAZELTON   – deal with it gracefully?

EILEEN   Not so much gracefully. Comfortably. I want her to feel good about it.

DR. BRAZELTON   Then you're talking about self-image, not social skills.

EILEEN   Exactly.

Eileen and Barry are already so attached to Jenny. Their real worry, more than what she would be like, is would she be really theirs?

DR. BRAZELTON   What you're both saying is, you'd like her to be yours, and to feel good about it. A lot of what she'll be is going to be due to you two, certainly. And what she'll think about herself will certainly have to come from you. This is the most critical thing you can give her.

EILEEN   What do you think of her, in terms of her personality and temperament?

DR. BRAZELTON   Do I think she's normal?

BARRY   Yes.

EILEEN   Do you think she's *wonderful*?

DR. BRAZELTON   I think she's incredible. She's not only lovely, but she's strong. She's very sensitive, and yet she's able to manage for herself, which is the best sign of internal stability. In addition, she's already showing a kind of inner fire. When she gets a chance to reach out and you respond and match what she's up to, she lights up.

THE ISSUES

It is impossible, of course, to predict what any small baby will be like in the future. All we can really do is see how the baby adjusts to her present situation. The style or temperament with which she manages her environment is our best clue to her future personality, although there are still many external life changes which can shape her future. In addition, each time a child moves to a new developmental stage, the way she takes on each new challenge – walking, talking, achieving autonomy – will give her an internal history, a set of experiences which will shape the way she approaches the world later.

Parents try hard to predict a baby's future and attach themselves to the merest hint of individual difference in a baby in their effort to understand her as a person. Each new bit of behavior is magnified in their minds. They personify any trait ("just like Grandma") in their effort to fit her into the world they know. The drive to see a baby as more mature than she really is ("She's already saying, 'Daddy'") is part of this same effort. If parents feel that they can predict a baby's future, they feel less anxious about that future. Every parent worries unconsciously about losing a baby. The more attached they become, the more they worry.

For adoptive parents like Barry and Eileen, this urge to know a child and the associated anxiety are accentuated. Every parent has a deep-seated urge to understand a new baby, to become important to her, to shape her future; but in adoptive parents these urges are even fiercer. The desire to predict a child's future is fueled by all the unknowns of the adopted baby's past, including the intrauterine experiences and what happened during any placement in a foster home.

In a cross-racial adoption, parents soon wonder about genetic differences. In my own research with newborns on four continents,

I have observed and demonstrated very subtle differences in the behavior, motor activity, and reactions to stimuli of black, Asian, and Caucasian babies. In these studies, I used the test I designed, the Brazelton Neonatal Behavioral Assessment Scale. This scale consists of a twenty-minute assessment of a newborn's reactions to voice, face, rattle, bell, red ball, to handling, to being cuddled, to being soothed when crying, and basic reflex and motor activity. There is a powerful universality in the human newborn. But there are differences in style, in the quality of alertness, of motor behavior, of responses to being handled and played with. These are individual differences to which parents will respond, and which will be likely to shape the parents' images of their babies. Black babies in western Kenya demonstrate vigorous motor activity, which in turn seems to elicit vigorous handling from their parents. Although they were just as alert to visual and auditory signals as babies from other cultures, motor activity seemed to be the most exciting and rewarding interactional medium for baby and parent. Everyone plays actively with small babies in Kenya; when they fuss, they are bounced vigorously to quiet them. Thus, the babies' inborn style seems to help set the tempo of the parents' reaction to them. White U.S. babies are not so vigorous.

Newborns in Japan and China are qualitatively different. For instance, on the delivery table, after a normal, nonmedicated delivery, a Japanese newborn from a peasant culture (I made these observations on the Goto Islands off the western coast of Japan) would lie quietly beside her mother. Her arms and legs would cycle quietly and her fingers would move delicately. These motions were smooth and without startles. As she lay there, she looked around and listened. If we offered her a low-key visual and auditory stimulus such as a soft rattle or a quiet voice, she would turn her head gently to search for the sound. She would follow my face back and forth, up and down, for prolonged periods of as much as twenty or thirty minutes, getting more and more alert as she followed. In these babies, visual and auditory interactions seemed most important. When we observed child-rearing practices in the households of these newborns, we noted that the adults offered gentle handling, soft voices, and quiet faces. It appeared that they respected these babies' need for low-key interactions. Their quiet, gentle nurturing was coupled with frequent breastfeeding to quiet newborns if they cried.

As I studied such qualitative differences from one culture to another, I saw both genetic and environmental influences at work. The genetic predisposition to certain kinds of motor responses and to a certain threshold for taking in and utilizing sensory stimuli has already been shaped during pregnancy by the mother's movements, the environment around her, and the quality of her reactions to this environment. In the quiet, primitive fisherman's villages on the Goto Islands, pregnant women are protected from too much stimulation. In Tokyo, where the pace of life and the level of stimulation is similar to that of U.S. cities, there is already a slight but definite difference in babies' behavior. They are still quieter and smoother in their movements than are Caucasian or black babies. Their periods of attention are still significantly longer than those of Caucasian babies in the U.S. But the Tokyo babies are closer to white U.S. babies in the quality of their responses than are the Goto Island babies. White U.S. babies move in a more jerky way, and are more easily distracted. They are more active, their motions interspersed with startles and jerky reflexes.

When I offer white babies in the United States an auditory or visual stimulus such as a talking face or a soft rattle, they move their heads to follow back and forth, up and down, but only for two or three minutes. As they try to attend longer, they have a reflex response of the whole body which breaks the cycle of attention. They must be soothed to start over again. U.S. Caucasian babies and Asian and African newborns have the same set of sensory and motor responses, but each seems to be *qualitatively* different. These individual differences, in turn, influence the parents' reactions.

As I handled Jenny, I was aware of her special style, I felt her low-key, smooth responses. She was gentle and quiet as I held her. I noticed that I could easily overload her by using a loud voice or by looking in her face in an intrusive way. She would gaze past me or turn away from me to cut me off. If I handled her abruptly or tried to toss her around, she would stiffen and arch, and then her whole body would go limp. Unless I respected her threshold for handling and for interaction, I would get no response from her. Her eyelids would begin to close down, her face would become immobile, and I knew I was out of contact with her. As I played with her, Eileen confirmed my observations. "I've had to learn not to be too exuberant with her. She certainly doesn't like it. I thought at first it was because she'd never been played with in her previous home, but I see that it's more her temperament."

I have noticed in my own practice that parents who make a cross-racial adoption must work harder than others to understand their baby and the qualitative difference in behavior in rhythms, in reactions, in motor behavior. When I tell mothers about my cross-cultural genetic work and how I'd come to believe that genetic differences need to be understood and respected, they are often delighted and relieved. "I thought at first that she didn't like me or my style of handling her." They tell me how, unconsciously, they have begun to fit their reactions to their babies. "Once I did, we began to know each other. It was quite an adjustment at first." Parents find that they must work hard to fit their style of response to their new baby's. At first, when this does not work, parents feel like failures. Some mothers compare it to a postpartum depression. In a way, they are right. Although they did not have the physical strain of making this baby, the psychological task of adjusting can be overwhelming. "No one told us about how hard it would be to learn about a three-month-old baby. Is it just that she's Korean?" (Or Colombian, or Vietnamese, and so on.)

Adoptive parents should be prepared in advance to expect and understand these differences. Otherwise, they will interpret the difficulties of adjusting to one another as their own lack of capacity to relate to a new baby. So deep-seated in each of us are our rhythms of movement, of interactive response, that we find it hard to adjust them when we make a relationship with someone who is different in style or temperament. New parents care so much that these differences take on magnified proportions and can even threaten the relationship they are trying to build. The natural anxiety and intensive effort of any new parent is exaggerated and can lead to depression if the feelings are buried. When cultural differences in the new baby's behavior can be shared with parents at the outset, they will not be blown out of proportion or misinterpreted. I hope that nurses, doctors, and other people who care for families with cross-cultural or cross-racial adoptions can become informed and sensitive to these issues.

While these adjustments are being made, parents will find that their adopted child's personality is gradually taking on aspects of their own personalities. Over time, she will begin to take on their attributes and blend their styles into hers. But under stress, such as a traumatic experience or a new adjustment such as school, when she must learn new things rapidly, the child's inborn temperamental style is likely to resurface. Then, she will need understanding and respect from her parents all over again. As she gets older, they can help her understand herself and her own temperamental style. It always surprises me to see how rewarding it is to a six- or seven-year-old child to begin to understand herself and her reactions. If Barry and Eileen can accept the differences between Jenny's temperament and their own, they will be ready to help her understand them as well. This growing mutual understanding will draw them closer and closer. Eileen and Barry's goal is to reach at the feeling that they are as close to her as they would have been to a natural child, and that nothing is missing – for her or for them.

COMMON QUESTIONS

QUESTION   Is a child more affected by genes or by the way her parents bring her up?

DR. BRAZELTON   Basic personality probably is inherited. But the way we use our assets and our temperament probably depends on environment and our experiences in facing stress. It is impossible *ever* to separate nature from nurture.

QUESTION   It seems like some behavior changes and some doesn't. Are there any rules?

The O'Connell-Beder Family

DR. BRAZELTON   Not simple ones. One reason that it is so hard to predict a child's future from behavior in infancy is that at each stage of development (and there are many), the child's whole personality is reorganized. This is good news, for it means that even with a fixed inheritance from a biological parent with severe problems, a child may learn to channel the same traits and use them as assets. Plasticity is the nature of the human organism. Learning from each of the stressful transitions of life, we keep changing and developing. Knowing this, an adoptive parent will be less likely to project the "sins" of the natural parent onto the child. To say "Just because her father was irresponsible, she's bound to be" seems grossly unfair, but it is a common fantasy of adoptive parents. The more you can back up the potential of your adopted child and the less you label him according to his background, the more you will add to his self-image and his ability to use any inherited patterns and traits in a positive way.

QUESTION   My daughter is quiet and sensitive, and also seems artistically inclined. Since I'm an artist, I'm hoping that she will continue to be that way. Is that something that we should encourage?

DR. BRAZELTON   Absolutely. Not only because she seems to have an artistic temperament, but especially because she can identify with you and your interests. She will sense and value your talent and feel reinforced by it. Don't push her, but support her when she tries to "be like Mommy."

What Will My Child Be Like?

QUESTION   My son is so easygoing now. Does that mean that when he gets older, people will start walking all over him?

DR. BRAZELTON   Not necessarily. An easygoing child can also be stubborn, determined, and secure. He can be laid back because he has an inner sense of himself. When he gets walked on, don't dive in to protect him. If you see his easygoing nature as a problem, he will see it as a failure in himself. If he is being bullied, say to him, "You know very well you can take care of yourself when you need to. You can learn to deal with bossy people. When you want to stand up to him, you can. When you do, he'll leave you alone. But if it doesn't bother you, it doesn't bother me. I know you can take care of yourself." A sense of security is what he will need to protect himself.

QUESTION   My daughter goes to a sitter three days a week, and when we leave her there, she doesn't seem to mind at all that we're leaving. She also takes her bottle by herself. She won't allow us to give it to her, and I wonder if this is a sign of independence she will have all of her life.

DR. BRAZELTON   I hope so. She sounds very competent and sure of herself. I'd let her know how proud you are of her. But I wouldn't assume that she can be so competent all the time. I'd prepare her for the sitter, and I'd stay with her for a bit anyway. I'd also always hold her when she's taking her bottle. Any child who still needs a bottle needs a period of closeness with you. If she regresses and does show a sudden need for more dependence, grab the opportunity and welcome it. Let her know it's OK to be dependent, even if she is so good at being independent.

QUESTION   How much of what we notice in our children is what we want them to become?

DR. BRAZELTON   Probably a good deal. The influence of our expectations is very powerful. A child will try hard, both consciously and unconsciously, to live up to your hope for him. So you will be shaping him all the time by your dreams. There is a cost to this. The child will strive to live up to your expectations and will even incorporate them into his own goals for himself. If he can make it, fine. If he can't, it may cost him a good self-image. So, you must constantly readjust your dream to reality by listening to what he wants to become and can become. If you can match your dreams with his own, you'll give him the best chance to feel good about himself.

QUESTION   Is there any relationship between physical development and verbal development? My daughter's speech is developing much earlier than her coordination.

DR. BRAZELTON   There seems to be an inverse relationship, at least in early speech development. A very active child doesn't seem to have time to speak. She must keep going. A less physically driven child is more likely to use speech to achieve what she wants.

QUESTION   On both sides of the family, we have a problem with overweight. It's something we have discussed with our pediatrician and are conscious

What Will My Child Be Like?

of. How likely is it that my son will also have a problem with overweight as he gets older?

DR. BRAZELTON   Quite likely. The body type of parents is very likely to be dominant and heritable. It doesn't always follow, for there are recessive genes which can appear. But it would be surprising if he didn't have a body type like yours. So it is important for him to learn weight control early. It won't happen by your manipulating him and what he eats. That is more likely to cause rebellion in him and overeating in the long run. He will learn by modeling himself on your behavior. If you can learn to watch your diet, without making an issue out of it, in all likelihood he'll mimic you. If you can set an example in activity and sports, he is more likely to value these. The combination of a controlled diet and regular sports is the surest way to avoid obesity.

QUESTION   My daughter has a tendency to be very aggressive with other children. She may be trying to give them a hug, but she ends up knocking them down. Does this mean she'll be aggressive as she gets older?

DR. BRAZELTON   I hope not. It needn't lead to aggression. She doesn't mean it now. However, if her approach frightens other children and their reaction in turn frightens her, patterns of anxious overreaction may get started. This might lead her to bully other children. I'd certainly help her to see that other children don't like roughness. I'd warn her before you go somewhere exciting that you'd like to help her find ways to control herself. And I'd practice them with her. Don't overreact when she fails, but do let her

The O'Connell-Beder Family

know you won't allow her to hurt others, and even remove her from the situation, if necessary. One of the best ways to help her will be to find another child just like her and let them play together. They'll learn rapidly from each other. Then you can help her learn how to approach less aggressive children. It's not that you should quell any aggression in her, but you can help her channel it into acceptable behavior, so that she will be liked by others and can like herself. Learning how to live with and control aggressive feelings is a lifelong process. If a child is afraid of getting out of control, she is more likely to hold back and then explode, and to become an uncomfortably aggressive person.

What Will My Child Be Like?

The O'Connell-Beder Family Revisited

ॐ

As I arrived at Eileen and Barry's small two-story house in a Boston suburb, I looked up the steep stairway to the porch above. Standing there to greet me were three of the family: Eileen, Barry, and three-year-old Jenny. A neighbor who was passing by saw me looking at them. "What a pretty picture!" she said. I had to agree. They are a striking trio. Eileen, with her strawberry blond hair and huge blue eyes, is a magazine editor's ideal of beauty. But she sparkles with warmth and welcome as well. Barry's dark, trim looks project quiet strength. Then Jenny, with her square body, her fine Asian features and straight black hair, becomes a third contrast. Her black eyes look wary as you approach. Each of them greeted me from the porch, but Jenny drew back to hide behind her parents' legs. She stared at me stonily for the first fifteen minutes after I arrived, not allowing me close to her. I turned away to talk to her cordial parents.

After we'd entered their house and had sat down at the table so that I could take notes, I felt a soft hand on my leg. Jenny was making a bid for my attention. As soon as I responded, she began to communicate. As if we'd lifted a floodgate, she began to show me her toys, to draw for me, to tell me her "secrets." For the rest of the visit, she acted as if I were there for her, and kept busy charming me. She chattered almost incessantly. Whenever I began to get immersed in conversation with her parents, her chatter became insistent, as if she were determined to keep adult attention. I wondered whether this wasn't her way of competing with John, her eighteen-month-old brother, who was asleep in another room.

Eileen told me that Jenny was famous for charming all their friends. I could believe it. When her delightful chatter failed, she'd insinuate herself physically. She would glide up to my knee, gently put her hand on my leg, and look piercingly at me with her dark eyes. I found her irresistible. I could hardly keep from either picking her up or leaning over to talk to her. It was difficult to converse with her parents. The moment I responded to her, she became quietly animated. Cocking her head slightly, she looked directly at me, smiling broadly, a dimple in her left cheek. She talked in full sentences, complicated ones for a three-year-old. Later, I realized how much she was like Eileen in her charm, both compelling and sophisticated. It was almost as if she were an Asian version of her mother's smiling Irish charm. The contrast between their looks made this likeness astonishing.

Before long, I found myself enthralled with them all. Barry's reserved, intelligent style was the anchor of this trio. Jenny's wooing of me told me how secure she was with him. In my office, I can soon tell how a child relates to her father by the way she deals with me. As we communicated, she began to settle cozily into our new relationship. She showed self-assurance, as well as a sense of joy, which I began to feel with her as well. The way a small child relates to a male physician or male family friend is almost always based on her past experience with the important man in her life. Children whose fathers are really involved with them grow up with a sense of trust which I can sense even in my brief contacts in the office.

Eileen told me about their life now. They adopted John fifteen months ago from the same Korean adoption agency that sent them Jenny. He, too, was three months old when he came over. The foster family who'd cared for him sent them pictures of themselves with him as a newborn, his teddy bear, and Korean costumes for him to wear when he was a few years older. They urged the Beders to send them pictures of him as he grew. The fact that he'd been with people who cared about him gave Eileen and Barry a good feeling.

Eileen is working only one day a week now, seeing patients in psychotherapy. She's a homemaker the rest of the time. Barry stays home two days a week to be with his family. The Beder Health Clinic, which runs programs for businesses and for individuals who want to stop smoking or drinking, as well as for other kinds of personal crisis management, is besieged with consulting work. Barry used to travel a great deal before the children came. Now he rarely leaves home.

Together, Barry and Eileen are working on a videotape to demonstrate some of his ideas and techniques for giving up smok-

The O'Connell-Beder Family Revisited

ing. He has combined self-hypnosis and other self-management maneuvers in an original way. The feeling of quiet assurance which he conveys must be a factor in the success of his clinic. He glows most, however, when he talks of his family. As he spoke about how difficult it was for him to let John invade his relationship with Jenny, I realized that I'd rarely heard fathers expose their deeper feelings like this. He said, "I need to be home extra time right now to sort out these new relationships with Jenny and John and even a new one with Eileen. We've never been happier." Eileen nodded.

They both now felt comfortable talking with me about what the infertility had really meant to them. Eight years of trying every month had left Eileen exhausted. The worst part for both of them was the lack of a diagnosis. The doctors all said there was absolutely no reason, and it still might happen anytime. They'd been through every possible test repeatedly, as well as surgery. They had tried temperature charts coupled with "orders to have sex in certain ways." Both had undergone every sort of procedure to visualize the reproductive tract. "They even made me have sex with a hamster egg," said Barry with a smile, "to be sure my sperm were potent." They are still trying. Eileen is on thyroid pills even though there's no real indication for this. The desperation behind their years of experimentation contrasted with the appearance of these handsome, self-assured people. I felt that the experiences had no doubt deepened their relationship and added to their self-awareness. The struggle had not been in vain.

"No one can identify the defect in either of us," said Eileen. "This should be reassuring, but it's not. It's just a tease. In fact, before we adopted Jenny, I was going crazy waiting each month; I built up to a crisis before each period. Each month, the disappointment and the letdown when my period started was so terrible that I was getting frantic. Our marriage was about to go. We were in therapy, trying to save it. Each of us blamed the other, and we blamed ourselves. Barry was traveling all the time. I was working frantically. We could see that we were living for a pregnancy, not for anything else. Although I still can't give up my longing to become pregnant, I began to see that I had to bring closure to part of my life. Even if I'd never be pregnant, I had to be a mother.

The O'Connell-Beder Family

So that's when we decided to adopt. We needed to save ourselves and to save our marriage, and it has."

I asked whether she wanted more children. She nodded. "Two is enough for me." said Barry. "I want time to enjoy the ones we have. I'm having enough trouble giving up on my special relation with Jenny." He paused and went on, "I come from a Boston Jewish family. My only brother was two and a half years older. We were always in competition, as I remember it. He had two boys; Michael, who is thirteen, loves us and wants to be in our family. He was really jealous of Jenny when we got her. We take him on our family outings. You see, my brother died two years ago of a brain tumor. It had been growing since he was young, probably. Maybe it had been there all along when everyone thought he was an underachiever. No one recognized he had such a problem until he was grown and had a family." I sensed his deep identification with his brother and his guilt over having been so competitive and of having "won." For he is indeed a success in his business, in his new family, and even in handling the problem of infertility. This sense of competition has undoubtedly fueled his success, but he still feels at some level that he contributed to his brother's tragedy. Such feelings, called "ghosts in the nursery" by child psychoanalyst Selma Fraiberg, remain as remnants from our past, and are bound to influence our reactions in ways over which we often have no control. Barry's awareness of his own feelings does give him a chance to control them, but not to be rid of them.

As they exposed their backgrounds, Eileen and Barry helped me understand why it was critical for them to become "nurturers." "At first I just couldn't accept myself as not being able to be pregnant," said Eileen. "If I couldn't be pregnant, I didn't want a baby at all. But I was more and more depressed and isolated from Barry, and I realized I was blaming him for it. I couldn't face taking the blame on myself. Look at my brother and sister — fertile! I must be."

"Meanwhile," said Barry, "I became angrier and angrier that she couldn't be fulfilled by just me. Why did she need a family, too? Wasn't I enough? I began to realize I couldn't tolerate the self-blame I was feeling."

The O'Connell-Beder Family Revisited

"One night," said Eileen, "I just decided, 'I've had it.' I can even remember where I was sitting and what the room looked like. I said to Barry, 'We're going to adopt.'" Barry nodded.

"For me," said Barry, "It was a matter of someone carrying on the name, the heritage. In Jewish families, that's important. *Now* my family is as thrilled with them as they are with my brother's children. But it wasn't that way at first. Also, I do still wonder about white babies with blue eyes. We both have blue eyes, and [looking at his wife] I even wonder about a baby with red-blond hair!"

"I keep saying now that I've proved myself as a mother," said Eileen, "and I've regained an important part of my ego. But I'm still driven to get pregnant. We have had our two perfect babies. I feel now I really like Jenny and John as people. Whenever I think of a baby of my own, I remind myself of how great they are. I'm not sure we'd ever have produced anyone as nice as Jenny or as exciting as John. Jenny came to us as a complete, competent little person. She waited a long time to talk our language, as if she couldn't give up on her Korean heritage. At two, she started. She began to talk in sentences. By two and a half, she was saying everything. She waits until she can do something, then does it perfectly. She is such a sweet person, so eager to please. She wants to do just what we want of her. We don't deserve her."

"Do you mean she came ready-made, and you couldn't ruin her?" I asked. Other adoptive parents have spoken this way.

Eileen nodded. "John is so different. He's already fallen downstairs three times. He pulled the plug covers off the wall sockets, and even loosened the sockets themselves. He lives dangerously; it's always exciting. When we took him into court to adopt him, he knocked all the ashtrays off the tables, looked up at the judge, and laughed provocatively. We felt the judge was looking at us to see whether we really could handle him. I was afraid he'd refuse the adoption. But, fortunately, he knew toddlers and their negativism."

"You talk of them as if they were opposites," I observed, "as if they were already strong individuals – even without you."

"I got the children of my dreams," said Eileen. "They do have strong personalities. They are good people. I like who they are. I watch them proudly when we're with other people. Everyone likes

The O'Connell-Beder Family

them. Jenny is already very popular with other children. I look forward to each stage of their development. The older they are, the better."

"Does this mean you're glad they're not babies anymore?" I asked.

"I'm not a baby person," she replied. "My pediatrician said maybe it has to do with their being adopted. He speculates that nine months of pregnancy allows adjustment to begin in a way that adoption doesn't."

I wondered whether it wasn't easier to feel responsible for them after they'd gotten older. I remembered again how tough it had been when Jenny first came, and mentioned this to Eileen. "Yes," she said, "I couldn't reach her, and I felt devastated. Then you suggested that I let Jenny come to me on her own time. I realized that I had been too overwhelming. She was *so* quiet, and I'm so exuberant. I relaxed and slowed down and she became more and more open. Just like she is now!" She looked proudly at Jenny.

Jenny came over to me. "Would you like some tea?" she said. "I'd *love* some tea!" I exclaimed. My enthusiasm seemed to worry her, and she said cautiously, "It's only betend tea." I realized that I'd responded too fast. I said quietly, "Jenny, betend tea is my favorite tea. I want your betend tea most of all." She grinned with her beautiful dimples. We proceeded to drink "betend" tea with real crackers, provided by her mother. I understood why Eileen and Barry had to work to respect their child's sensitivity. She still could easily be overwhelmed by too strong a response. After this episode, in which I had respected her need for a less dramatic interchange, she was mine. She sat on my lap. She looked around to listen to whatever I said, played quietly when we asked her to, and responded with complex answers when I asked her a question. Now we were truly friends and "on the same wavelength."

"How did you decide to adopt an Asian baby?" I asked her parents. "Did you try in this country?"

"Oh, yes," said Eileen. "We went through the hoops. You can't imagine what it's like these days to try to locate a baby."

"When Eileen went to the Catholic Charities," asked Barry, "they said, 'We can't give you a Catholic baby. You're married to a Jew. How do we know what religion this baby would be raised

The O'Connell-Beder Family Revisited

in?' When she applied to Jewish agencies, they said, 'We never give our babies to a mother who is not Jewish. Even if the father is Jewish. It's the mother's faith that matters.'"

"When we went to the South American sources," Eileen continued, "we found out what a terrible black market that can be. You send a thousand dollars just to register as a prospect. Then you may never hear from them again. We've had friends get as far as going down there to find that there's no baby available. It bothers us to have babies treated as chattel. We couldn't stand that, so we gave up on Latin America. We'd been to China and seen how wonderful their babies were, and we thought why not an Asian baby?"

"We felt immediately comfortable with the agency we went to here in Massachusetts." Barry went on. "They put us in touch with the foster parents. They prepared us for the baby's arrival. They acted as if the *baby* and her adjustment was their goal. Not just money, or pleasing us. We immediately felt that our interests were like theirs. We all wanted the best for the baby."

I noticed pictures of Chinese people and of China on several of their walls. I asked whether this was a conscious effort on their part to make the children aware of their heritage and of other people like them. Barry said quietly, "No. They are from a trip. Actually we've thought of taking them down for fear of their being confused by them."

"Confused?" I asked.

"They might wonder if these are their family," Barry explained. "Friends said they would grow up thinking these were their family, since they look so different from us. The people in the pictures look like them."

"But they need to understand the differences," I replied. "They will need to know they're not from your genes."

"What I plan to say," said Eileen, "is that 'Daddy and I aren't born into the same family. We are from different backgrounds. We chose each other to be a family. That's the way we chose you. We are a family, all from different backgrounds.'"

"That's a great way to say it. I wouldn't ever give up on the concept of 'This is your family,'" I urged. "They'll need to hear you say it. But they also need to have Asian people to identify with. That's why pictures, the Asian touches in your house, as well as John's costumes, are so great."

"We've joined a group of other parents who are raising Asian children," said Eileen. "There is a large group of us now. Our children all see each other, and we learn so much from each other. They're all talking about a third adoption. It makes me feel we should, too."

Barry winced. "No more!" he exclaimed.

"Unless I get pregnant," said Eileen. Barry nodded.

Neither of them had quite given up on the dream of Eileen becoming pregnant. I hoped they never would give up their dream – as long as it didn't cost them too much.

"I wanted to tell you about a game Jenny played right after she'd learned to talk," said Eileen. "She'd say, 'I'm a doctor.' I'd say, 'Do you want to go to the doctor?' She'd shake her head. 'No. I *am* a doctor!' We were puzzled until, one day, she said, 'I'm a doctor when I was a baby.' I realized she'd been trying to get me to understand that she knew about being adopted."

Here was the answer to one of the questions adoptive parents always have: When should I tell her she's adopted? If you talk about it from the first, it's an accepted part of her. Jenny was trying to get the reassurance that Eileen, too, accepted it. This will happen from time to time and needs to be met with absolute assurance.

"Just the other day," Eileen continued, "she said, 'Are you my real mother?' I think it came at a time when we were at a public swimming place. When I called her, the other kids saw how different looking we were and they asked her about it. 'Is that your *real* mother?' Jenny looked anxious, not about the question but about being teased. I said, 'Of course, I'm your real mother!' She said, 'But I came on a plane.' 'Yes, but you came for me to be your real mother. Someone in Korea who couldn't be a real mother to you let me have you to be my child and part of my family. Now, Daddy and I *are* your real family.' She subsided, rushed back to tell them, 'She *is* my real mommy!' We hear her explaining all this to them. I guess it's going to happen over and over the older she gets."

"People are always asking us, 'Are they brother and sister?'" added Barry. Someone even said, 'Are they twins?' It seems so

The O'Connell-Beder Family Revisited

insensitive to us that people think Asian children all look alike. It seems as if people don't even look. We love their individuality."

"Unfortunately, they will have to face it over and over," I said. "They do look different from the children around them. At school, that will bother other children who will be sorting out their own individual differences. Your role will be to reassure them of their individuality, of the importance of their background and their culture, but also of their complete acceptance here within your family."

"I've already dealt with the difference between us as a Catholic and a Jew. Our families had a hard enough time with our marriage: 'Will you circumcise your boys? Will you baptize your babies?' We had to help them with those adjustments, and in the process, we came to understand our own feelings about differences. Now we are better prepared to help the kids."

"Do your families accept them now?" I asked.

"Oh, yes," said Eileen. "They call about them all the time. My sister's son is one month apart from John in age, and my brother has a daughter two weeks younger than Jenny. Jenny will be going to the same school as her cousin. They are devoted to each other. They are very much a part of our extended family, and the kids are devoted to each other."

"They are indeed lucky children," I said.

"Well, we're lucky, too," said Barry. "They've really cemented our family. We go around as a pack now – four of us as a group. We've never been happier together – Eileen and I. We feel a sense of fulfillment I'd never dreamed of." Eileen nodded vigorously. "I stay home two working days, clean the house, and do some cooking – to help Eileen, but also to be a real part of the family."

"His male friends are very threatened by this," Eileen said with a smile. "They call and say, 'Would you clean our house, too?' or 'Cut it out – you're getting us into trouble.' They are really threatened."

"It doesn't bother me anymore," said Barry. "It did at first, I must admit. But I realized that when we found we couldn't have a baby, it hit me very deep. I began to wonder whether it was meant to be. Maybe I wasn't given a baby because I couldn't nurture. Maybe I wasn't OK. On the way to the airport to get

Jenny, I was still wondering, 'Am I OK to be someone's father?' Now, I'm very proud of being a good father. It more than makes up for any failure. John calls us both Mama."

"If I'm not home for a few days," Barry went on, "I forget where things are. I *need* to be here for my own sake, to keep my hand in. The only time I feel torn is when Eileen calls me at the office, when I'm running a session with a high-powered group of executives. She calls and says, 'The children want to talk to you!' I have to stop to talk children's talk. But I know what rewards I've gotten from all of this, so I figure these executives could take a lesson from it themselves."

Meanwhile, Jenny was crawling up into my lap, her jam-covered fingers exploring my face, determined to know all she could about me. I commented on how secure she feels about men. Barry said proudly, "We have such a good time together. We play for an hour at a time. I get a real high from playing with her."

"Does the high worry you?" I asked. "Today, everyone worries so much about sexual feelings, about abuse, that some fathers feel inhibited when they play with their daughters."

"Well," said Barry, "I do feel slightly uneasy when she crawls into bed with me. After my psychiatric training, it's hard not to be self-conscious when she says things like, "I like your penis!" But I *know* down deep how secure and clear our relationship is, so I'm not really threatened by it. I see it as her way of knowing me better. I hope I don't pass on any sense of embarrassment."

"She's such a direct little girl," added Eileen. "She said the other day, 'I don't like this baby anymore. Send him back on the plane. I want to be your only doctor child!'"

"She is such a blessing," Barry went on. "She's made me feel personally intact again. And she's put our marriage on an entirely different basis. We could have drifted apart so easily in all that stressful period. Now we are committed to each other at an entirely different level. I see Eileen as a good mother. She sees me as a good father. It gives us a whole new level of assurance. We are happier than ever now."

Jenny began to show off. She did a cartwheel. She jumped high. She showed a kind of physical talent and coordination which I've seen before in China in the children there who are training in acrobatics. They are so well coordinated that it is stunning to watch them move and perform. John, who now appeared from his nap, followed right behind, imitating her every movement, with early signs of the same coordination and motor ability that Jenny has.

Eileen and Barry proudly talk about these noticeable gifts and want to foster them. They want to introduce Jenny to some training, but they have run into a kind of stubborn resistance in her. "*I* want to do it," she says when anyone tries to show her anything about acrobatics. They will have to introduce her to lessons carefully. I sense that they want her to develop this special skill as a way of helping her face the teasing about differences that she will get from her peers. However, she must be ready for lessons, and not pushed into a learning situation. At some later point, she may well show a hunger for instruction and more skill. Musicians have told me that a talented child is usually ready for lessons and for the discipline of practicing by the age of five or six, but not before. Jenny must first develop a sense of her own talent, of things she can do well, by herself. Then, she will be receptive to a sensitive teacher, who can help her develop this talent. Barry and Eileen's admiration and joy in her beautiful coordination will reinforce it enough at this time. I encouraged them to wait for signs of readiness in her.

It's all too easy to push a three-year-old child to learn a new skill – such as acrobatics or reading or writing. If Eileen and Barry started her on lessons now, she'd learn. I've seen children who learned to read and write at three and four years, or to perform physically or musically at this age. They are trying to please the adults around them. But they aren't necessarily getting an inner pleasure from this learning. As Jenny says, "*I* want to do it." When they are older, this kind of early training may even interfere with learning. Precocious learning patterns don't always generalize to later, more complicated learning patterns. A child like Jenny will get more inner satisfaction from playing and exploring different uses of her body in spontaneous antics. Play is a child's way of learning. While playing, children are always experimenting. They drop the techniques which don't work and continue to improve the ones that do. If Eileen and Barry pushed her to learn now, her own inner excitement about mastering her body might be submerged. Eileen and Barry would do well to respect Jenny's stubborn refusal and to foster her learning via play and in interaction with her peers, rather than with adult teachers. A child's job in the preschool years is to learn about herself, not to learn to compete or to learn complex skills that can come later.

As I was preparing to leave, Jenny became a bit more clinging, as if she didn't want me to go. She led me upstairs to her bedroom, where she showed a picture and said proudly, "That's me and *you!*" She was right. There was a picture someone took in my office of me, and of her as a baby with Eileen and Barry. We were smiling and looking down at this serious, new baby who'd just been flown in from the Orient. She was watching us all worriedly as we overreacted, trying to reach her. I realized how sensitively, and how far, Eileen and Barry had come in adjusting to this lovely girl. At three, she was already outgoing, self-assured, and thoroughly at home.

When to Seek Help

❧

CHAPTER VI

੭ֆ

The universal question which arises in a crisis is "Why me?" The answer, of course, is that it's not just you. *Every* family faces crises. Learning to live with the stress they bring is maturity. Stress can either undermine or strengthen a family. In writing this book, I have tried to convey certain of the ways families can learn and grow as they confront threatening, tragic, or overwhelming situations. I've also searched for the particular attitudes or strengths which tipped the scale toward successful coping. Families faced by loss, stress, or illness can wallow in self-pity or become stuck in defense and denial. If a family feels itself drawn in that direction, outside help can tip the balance back again. Several of the families in this book found therapy helpful, and all the families drew on informal help and support from relatives, friends, or physicians.

How can parents tell when their response to stress is becoming destructive and when outside help is needed? An understanding of universal adaptive strategies, whether of individuals or of families, will reassure parents when they are on course, and alert them when help may be needed.

A useful notion for families trying to deal with stress of any kind is the recognition that the *stressor* (or event causing the stress) is neutral. Whether a family or individual adapts or grows in response to an outside event depends not so much on the nature of the event as on the resources and vulnerabilities within that family. These strengths and weaknesses cannot be firmly predicted ahead of time. In other words, one can't tell from the severity of the problem or disruption whether a family will need help. One family can come through an illness or loss with new solidarity, while another will be devastated by the same event. In deciding whether help is needed, self-observation and listening to feelings of other members of the family are more useful than analyzing or labeling the stress. Past experience, economic situation, ethnic background, and family relationships, among other influences, will determine each individual's interpretation of a challenge, which in turn determines whether it is manageable or not.

My experience in observing both children and families over thirty-five years has taught me that a family's responses to crisis or to a new situation mirror those of the child. That is to say, the way a small child deals with a new challenge (for instance, learning to walk) has certain predictable stages: regression, anxiety, mastery, new energy, growth, and feedback for future achievement. These stages can also be seen in adults coping with new life events, whether positive or negative. The challenge of dealing with an adoption, divorce, illness, or other shifts in circumstances calls up predictable stages of response in all of us. Just as a baby achieves a new balance and sense of self after mastering a skill, so a family works toward a new stability after handling a crisis. Both individuals and families must be flexible enough to adapt and become transformed, but also strong enough to maintain an identity and secure attachments.

For families or individuals, regression is often an early response to change. Children regress just before they take a major spurt in development. Thumbsucking, bedwetting, sleep problems can arise. In the midst of this regression, children appear to be disintegrated – babyish, overly dependent, anxious, fearful. At the time, these responses in a previously cheerful and enterprising child can seem frightening. Later, they can be seen as conservative strategies, ways to protect time and space until new energy and ways of adapting can be found. Young Charles Cooper could be seen regressing in this way before recovering from the death of his mother.

Families regress, too. In the face of a new situation or loss, families can become disorganized, tense, conflicted. A family may need to fall apart in order to call up alarm reactions in the individual members, to mobilize everyone for the new challenge. Eileen O'Connell and Barry Beder spoke of the strains that arose between them before they rallied in the face of infertility and decided to adopt. This regressive period may be frightening, for it is likely to uncover weaknesses and defects in the family as a system. Before the stress, everything may have looked and felt fine – on the surface. It is only under stress that we become aware of underlying rivalries, fears, weak links in family attachments. For each member of a family, this is a period of doubt and confusion: Can I muster enough energy to meet the new demands? Can we as a family ever band together to offer each other the strength we will need? Despite the pain and discomfort of such a period, a kind of emotional adrenaline courses through the family, and this very sense of disorganization makes room for growth and change.

After the first shock, there is often a period of disbelief or denial as we saw in the McClay family. After a severe loss, members of a family may be depressed, unable to eat or sleep, prone to cry unexpectedly and uncontrollably, unable to act or react. Physical symptoms may also appear. Children and adults are more vulnerable to infections at such a time.

As the initial numbness lifts, worries about the new situation will emerge. Irrational fears may surface. Familiar activities such as driving a car may seem frightening. Children develop fear of the dark, or of separation, or they wake with nightmares. They may refuse to go to school or leave the household. Another common feeling is guilt: What did I do or not do to allow this to happen? Were my aggressive or resentful wishes the cause? Did I do enough to prevent it? Children of three through six, especially, are prey to irrational fantasies. They fear that they have caused the illness or divorce. They try to become impossibly good. They are likely to take on more responsibility than they can handle – and then to give in later to a feeling of helplessness. Adults in a family will also feel guilt, will try to become models of fortitude and strength in a way that cannot be sustained.

After these periods of denial, fear, and guilt, withdrawal can occur. If the child or the family sees the situation as too overwhelming, a sense of helplessness may set in. Children with a quiet, sad appearance, those who appear to please everyone but seem emotionless, those who do not appear to react to physical or emotional pain may be defending themselves against stress by withdrawal. Families can also retreat into a tense, aloof world of their own if the individual members feel helpless in an ongoing crisis. We saw this in the McClay family, who "circled the wagons" and pulled back into themselves, without energy for any activity outside the family, while young Kevin was going through chemotherapy.

When to Seek Help

Many of these reactions to a crisis – regression, denial, fear, and withdrawal – are healthy, adaptive ones in that they allow the child and the family time and space to muster energy and feel their way toward a new balance. It is only when the child or family gets stuck that these reactions become destructive rather than helpful.

In each of the families in this book, we have seen how overcoming a crisis eventually leads to a stronger family system. When a child achieves a new level of development, a sense of competence fuels the child's self-image. This same pattern can be seen in families. Like a child mastering a new skill, the family which successfully weathers the divorce, illness, or other storm feels exhilarated, confident: "We did it!" The experience of transcending a stressful event becomes a force for strengthening the whole family.

At some point, however, many families find that they are going in circles and unable to get on with their lives. One or more of the normal reactions described above takes over. The situation escalates and feels out of control. Sometimes the inevitable period of regression does not seem to pass, or the family struggles to deny the problem. Often someone outside the family – a teacher, pediatrician, day care worker, or friend – may comment on the tension and ask what is gong on. Most often, one individual in the family will feel depressed or completely overwhelmed. All these signals suggest that some sort of therapy or outside support may be a good idea.

In trying to judge whether the painful emotions or problems being experienced are normal and will pass with time, or whether to seek help, perhaps the most important signal is that of feeling *stuck*. Parents may notice that they are playing out certain issues over and over on one another, in a circular fashion. To those around them, the solution may appear to be obvious, but from within the family, the problem may seem hopeless, unsolvable.

In such a situation, a few sessions of therapy may feel truly eye-opening: "I don't *need* to be stuck in this bind!" Suddenly, the parents may see that "ghosts" from their own childhood are clouding their view, that emotions and fantasies having nothing to do with the present crisis are distorting their judgment.

The first line of possible help may be the pediatrician, family physician, or nurse practitioner who provides basic medical care for the family. As we have seen through the stories in this book, the process of openly airing a problem with an objective person outside the family may illuminate the issues, without the need for formal therapy. This primary caretaker may also refer parents to a support group of families in the same situation, such as Parents Without Partners, associations of stepparents, or groups for adoptive parents.

Some families will be fortunate enough to find a pediatrician who can offer what is called "anticipatory guidance." In preparing for a change such as the adoption planned by the O'Connell-Beder family and the Cutlers, the arrival of a new baby in a blended family, or the approach of adolescence in a single-parent family like the Coopers, it is of immense value to have as much information and backup as possible. A pediatrician can prepare a family beforehand for the stresses of such adjustments and can acquaint parents with what to expect and let them see their reactions as universal. He or she can prepare them for their own inevitable anxieties. By doing so, the physician also helps them recognize when their reactions get out of the normal range. With advance preparation, a family is in much better shape to handle a change.

If a crisis demands more resources than family members can muster, a supportive physician can participate in the decision of when and to whom to refer them for more intense help. The choice of possible therapists includes child and adult psychiatrists (who have a medical degree and training in psychiatry), clinical psychologists (who have a Ph.D. and practice psychotherapy), and social workers (whose degree is usually at the master's level – M.S.W. or L.C.S.W. – and who have specialized in psychiatric social work).

For families seeking help for a crisis or a problem affecting more than one member of the family, such as those described in this book, there is also a choice between individual therapy, for the child or one parent, or family therapy. The advice of a pediatrician or nurse, the parents' own sense of where the problem lies, and their intuitive preference for, or sense of comfort in, a group or individual situation will guide this choice.

Family therapy is a relatively new and rapidly advancing field. A skilled family therapist can assess the individual strengths and failures in each member, as they interact with each other. He or she will focus on the successes and previous strengths in the family and build on these to handle the present crisis. If the therapist appears to be most concerned with the failures, I would recommend seeking a more balanced person.

Therapy for an individual child should be considered when the child is frightened or withdraws and cannot be reached by the parents, or when emotional or psychosomatic symptoms interfere with his or her functioning – in school, with peers, or with siblings. If a child seems not to play actively, or to be enjoying it less, this can also be a warning sign. The great British child analyst D. W. Winnicott wrote that "if a child is playing, there is room for a symptom or two, and if a child is able to enjoy play, both alone and with other children, there is no very serious trouble afoot."* Another sign that a child needs help is the reactions of other children. If they consistently shy away, they are sensing the child's upset. He or she will, in turn, sense their rejection, and this can become a vicious cycle of isolation.

Therapy can be a major opportunity for the whole family to look backward to past achievements, to consolidate strengths, and to reorganize at a new level of fulfillment. Not only is it worth undertaking for the sake of holding the family together, but the repercussions of mastering a crisis will be felt years later by both parents and children. No family stands still. There will be change, either in the direction of disorganization and a narrowing of options or toward growth and greater solidarity. A brave and caring family like those in this book will do all that it takes to grow and move on.

---

* *The Child, the Family, and the Outside World* (Reading, Mass.: Addison-Wesley, 1987).

For Further Reading

⽞

THE INVOLVED FATHER AND PARENTAL RIVALRY

Bittman, S., and Zalk, S. *Expectant Fathers*. New York: Ballantine Books, 1981.

Brazelton, T. B. *Working and Caring*. Reading, Mass.: Addison-Wesley, 1985.

Ehrensaft, D. *Parenting Together*. New York: Free Press, 1987.

Galinsky, E. *The Six Stages of Parenthood*. Reading, Mass.: Addison-Wesley, 1987.

Greenberg, M. *The Birth of a Father*. New York: Crossroads/Continuum, 1985.

Lapinski, S., and Hinds, M. D. *In a Family Way*. Boston: Little, Brown, 1982.

Parke, R. *Fathers*. Cambridge, Mass.: Harvard University Press, 1981.

Pruett, K. *The Nurturing Father*. New York: Warner Books, 1987.

Robinson, B. E., and Barrett, R. L. *The Developing Father*. New York: Guilford Press, 1986.

GRANDPARENTING

Carter, L. *Congratulations – You're Going to Be a Grandmother*! La Jolla, Calif.: Oak Tree Press, 1980.

Kornhaber, A., and Woodward, K. L. *Grandparents/Grandchildren: The Vital Connection*. Garden City, New York: Doubleday, 1984.

Le Shan, E. *Grandparents: A Special Kind of Love*. New York: Macmillan, 1984.

LOSS OF A PARENT

Furman, E. *A Child's Parent Dies*. New Haven: Yale University Press, 1974.

Grollman, E. *Explaining Death to Children*. Boston: Beacon Press, 1967.

Grollman, E. *Talking about Death*. Boston: Beacon Press, 1970.

Krementz, J. *How It Feels When a Parent Dies*. New York: Knopf, 1983.

Jewett, C. *Helping Children Cope with Separation and Loss*. Cambridge, Mass.: Harvard Common Press, 1982.

Le Shan, E. *When a Parent is Very Sick*. New York: Atlantic Monthly Press, 1986.

FATHERING ALONE

Atlas, S. *The Parents Without Partners Handbook*. Philadelphia: Running Press, 1984.

Dodson, F. *How to Single Parent*. New York: Harper and Row, 1986.

Gathy, R. H., and Kouloch, D. *Single Father's Handbook*. Garden City, N.Y.: Doubleday, 1979.

STEPFAMILIES

Berman, C. *Making It as a Stepparent*. Garden City, N.Y.: Doubleday, 1986.

Goldstein, S., and Solnit, A. J. *Divorce and Your Child*. New Haven: Yale University Press, 1985.

Lofas, J., and Jova, D. B. *Stepparenting*. New York: Kensington Publishing, 1985.

Rosen, M. *Stepfathering*. New York: Ballantine Books, 1987.

Wallerstein, J. S., and Kelly, J. B. *Surviving the Breakup*. New York: Basic Books, 1980.

Wallerstein, J. S., and Blakeslee, S. *Second Chances*. New York: Ticknor and Fields, 1989.

ILLNESS IN THE FAMILY

Boston Children's Hospital. *The New Child Health Encyclopedia*. New York: Delacorte Press, 1987.

Jones, M. L. *Home Care for the Chronically Ill or Disabled Child*. New York: Harper and Row, 1985.

NOTE: For referrals to parent support groups, contact Children In Hospitals, 31 Wilshire Park, Needham, Mass. 02192. Also, The Association for the Care of Children's Health, 3615 Wisconsin Ave., Washington, D.C. 20016 publishes helpful brochures.

INFERTILITY

Glazer, E. S., and Cooper, S. L. *Without Child*. Lexington, Mass.: Lexington Books, 1988.

Silber, S. *How to Get Pregnant*. New York: Warner Books, 1981.

NOTE: For referrals to local support groups, contact Resolve, 5 Water Street, Arlington, Mass. 02174.

ADOPTION

Gilman, L. *The Adoption Resource Book*, revised edition. New York: Harper and Row, 1987.

Horman, E. *After the Adoption*. Old Tappan, N.J.: Fleming H. Revell, 1987.

Lifton, B. J. *Lost and Found*. New York: Harper and Row, 1988.

Plumer, J. E. *Successful Adoption*, revised edition. New York: Crown, 1987.

For Further Reading

Index

About the Author

T. Berry Brazelton, M.D., who was born and grew up in Waco, Texas, is Professor of Pediatrics at Harvard Medical School and chief of the Child Development Unit at the Boston Children's Hospital. The Brazelton Neonatal Behavioral Assessment Scale is in use in major hospitals throughout the United States and abroad. Dr. Brazelton was awarded the prestigious C. Anderson Aldrich Award for Outstanding Contributions to the Field of Child Development by the American Academy of Pediatrics, and the Woodrow Wilson Award by Princeton University. He is president of the Society for Research in Child Development and the National Center for Clinical Infant Programs. Aside from his numerous scholarly publications, he is well known to parents as a contributing editor of *Family Circle* magazine and as the host of the popular Lifetime television series "What Every Baby Knows," from which much of this book was drawn. Among Dr. Brazelton's many books are *Infants and Mothers, Toddlers and Parents, On Becoming a Family, Working and Caring,* and *To Listen to a Child.*